THE MAN WHO STOLE FIRST BASE

Tales From Baseball's Past

THE MAN WHO STOLE FIRST BASE

Tales From Baseball's Past

Eric Nadel and Craig R. Wright

Foreword
by
Bill James

Taylor Publishing Company
Dallas, Texas

Published by

Taylor Publishing Company
1550 West Mockingbird Lane
Dallas, Texas 75235

Except where otherwise credited, all photographs are courtesy of the National Baseball Library in Cooperstown, New York.

Book design by Lee Hendricks

Library of Congress Cataloging-in-Publication Data

Nadel, Eric.
    The man who stole first base: tales from baseball's past/Eric Nadel and Craig R. Wright: foreword by Bill James.
        p. cm.
    Includes index.
    ISBN 0-87833-633-8: $9.95
    1. Baseball — History. 2. Baseball — Anecdotes. I. Wright,
Craig R. II. Title.
GV 862.5.N33 1988   88-26706
796.357' 0207—dc19   CIP

Printed in the United States of America

10 9 8 7 6 5 4 3 2 1

To the memory of
Bill Veeck, Jr.
for kindnesses not forgotten

FOREWORD

The first thing we have to understand about baseball writing is that baseball exists to be enjoyed. The second thing we have to understand is that this changes all the other rules. Take journalism, for example, Now journalists, on occasion, can be right serious in how they approach their subjects, and they should be; it would not be appropriate to report on floods, fires, murder, and mayhem with your tongue in your cheek. Sports are different. Floods, fire, murder, and mayhem are not by their nature enjoyable.

There are two basic groups of sports journalists—those who understand this distinction, and who therefore report on sports in such a way as to help the sports fan enjoy them, and those who proceed from the paradigm of educational theory, and report on sports as if they were another subdivision of the catastrophes of modern society. From the one group you get arguments about MVP Awards, profiles and superstars, updates on the pennant race, humor, parody, history, trivia, speculation, and silliness. From the other, you get serious articles about drugs, payoffs, racism, gambling, dissension, greed, impending financial ruin, moral decay, tooth decay, and your occasional shoulder injury or social disease. Thank God for serious Americans; I don't know what sports would come to without them.

I am certainly not intent here upon alienating serious sports journalists or serious sports historians or serious sports anything; I've been accused of being serious myself on one or two occasions. I am saying, let us ponder the paradox of this book: that men as intelligent, as knowledgeable, as thorough, as...well, serious, in the best sense of the word, as Craig Wright and Eric Nadel would choose to do a radio show and write a book which is simply such a joy—so light and bright and generally cheery that at times it seems in danger of floating out of your hands. But I understand that paradox perfectly, perhaps only because I have so much in common with them. There was a pivotal moment in my evolution as a sportswriter, a moment which occurred in 1978 in the press box of a game in Kansas City, but which I think I have never written about. What happened first that day was that the two teams, the Royals and the Baltimore Orioles, played an absolutely fantastic baseball game—a gripping, wrenching, seesawing contest eventually won by Royals in their last at bat. What happened second was that *nobody in the press box noticed.* I looked around me, and I saw faces not drained or exhausted, not happy or sad, not relieved or frustrated. I saw men hunched over their modems typing furiously. "What an incredible game," I started to say to the man next to me, and as the words were half-formed on my face he turned to the man next to him and muttered, "The only good thing about this game is that it is over."

And that man muttered, "Yeah."

Now, by the lights of their profession, I should not even need to explain that these men were guilty of no oversight. The game ended at 10:30 and they had a 10:20 deadline; I didn't expect them to scratch their tummies for a half-hour before they filed their stories. But I was dumbfounded by the paradox: that this thing existed only to be enjoyed, and yet these men were, by the nature of their assignment, utterly incapable of enjoying it—nay, more; incapable even of perceiving what the game *was* to the fans in the stands. Objectivity is a God to journalism; the universal admonition against cheering in the press box is in effect an admonition not to enjoy the game in the way that a fan enjoys it. But I wondered about this: if a man sees a wonderful game, and he does not know that he has seen a wonderful game, can he really be said to have seen it objectively? Can he be said to be reporting objectively upon a thing which exists only to be enjoyed, if he has not the capacity to enjoy it? The very essence of the enterprise is excluded from his report.

If I had the time I should give you the newspaper accounts of that game; I will assure you that not one account, and I read four, so much as hinted that anything exceptional had occurred that night. Is not the good journalist, in a sense, like a poet who will not allow himself to smell the rose of which he rhapsodizes, for fear that the sensation might overpower his verse? Is that "objectivity," in fact, a protection of accurate perception, or a barrier to accurate perception?

The world is what it is; we cannot make it better by bewailing its inconsistencies. Of course sportswriters do not live under a perpetual deadline; most of them can and do enjoy those parts of the game which are open to them. But I decided that morning that I would never do that to myself; I would never put myself in a position from which I was unable to enjoy the moment of the contest. I would never become unwilling to enjoy the game, no matter what journalists thought of that.

And I understand, because of that, why Craig and Eric are able to do their radio show *A Page From Baseball's Past,* which has led to this book. They have struggled for most of their lives to understand this game a little better each day than the day before—yet each is also logical enough to understand that he must not *stop* enjoying the game as a part of his struggle to understand it, but rather must learn to enjoy it more, to enjoy it in more different ways.

Well, I love the book. We enjoy learning about baseball; that is part of the experience of the fan. People send me manuscripts all the time; this is the first one I'm going to get spiral-bound so I can keep it handy until the book comes out. Who can't love a book that tells you about teams like the Reading Railroad "Hoppers," an entire team made up of players left shy a limb by their employers, and their rivals, the Philadelphia Snorkies? Who can't love a book that actually helps you to understand better the 1951 Playoff Game, that tells you about the untimely death of a 21-year-old star of the Civil War era (whose team, incidentally, once beat an All-Star team of their opposition despite giving them 18 players in the field and six outs an inning)? Who can't love a book which tells you about the player who hit three home runs in an inning, a book which recounts the battle against players' smoking, a book which traces the history of the record for throwing a baseball the farthest? You're not a baseball fan if you can't love a book which tells you who the greatest batting practice pitcher of all time was. Why wouldn't you love a book which tells you about a player who practiced hitting a baseball while hanging upside down from a trapeze and catching flies in a jeep? In short, you're not a baseball fan if you can't love this book.

—Bill James

ACKNOWLEDGMENTS

There are literally hundreds of people who have assisted in the collection and research of these stories. Sometimes it's as small a part as Eddie Robinson holding his fingers an inch apart to show how close his foul line-drive came to ending Bobo Holloman's no-hitter before making the final out, or Bobby Bragan putting us in touch with George Sisler, Jr. for help in a show about his father. Loads of folks have shared ideas for shows or volunteered unknown details. Many of our stories have been rewritten two or three times over the years to bring out new information. Beyond the actual characters who make these stories happen —bless you Bill Veeck—the real heroes are the tireless researchers who have done so much to bring baseball's past to life for everyone: folks like Jim Baker, Bob Davids, Bill James, John Holoway, Lloyd Johnson, Al Kermisch, Vern Luse, Bob Tiemann, and other colleagues from the Society for American Baseball Research, as well as the ever helpful staff of the National Baseball Library in Cooperstown. One of the pleasures in doing this book is the opportunity to acknowledge your contributions. And last we thank those really responsible for making this project work. Thanks for listening and now thanks for reading.

E.N. and C.R.W.

The Man
Who Stole First Base

When batting coaches feel a base stealer is spending too much time on his running technique rather than his hitting, they often use the old saw, "You can't steal first base." They obviously never heard of Herman "Germany" Schaefer.

The stocky little second baseman played fifteen years in the majors despite being a mediocre ballplayer. He was good enough to play as a regular on back-to-back pennant winners with the Detroit Tigers in 1907–1908, but they didn't have any trouble taking a third pennant in 1909 after trading Schaefer to Washington.

Schaefer hit only .250 for Detroit, but that was pretty typical for the career .257 hitter. Old Herm stood out on those Tiger teams as the exact opposite of the team's star center fielder, the ultra-serious and mean-spirited Ty Cobb. Schaefer's value was as a player who could keep his team loose and having fun. Tiger teammate Davey

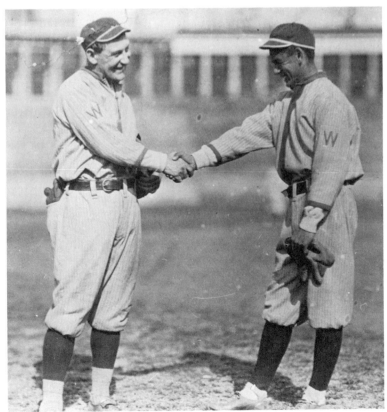

"Germany" Schaefer with Merito Acosta when both played for the Washington Senators in 1914.

Jones once claimed that Schaefer was the funniest man he'd ever seen, including Charlie Chaplin.

Davey Jones also happened to be the runner on third base when Schaefer made baseball history with his unique steal attempt. It happened in a game between Detroit and Cleveland on September 4, 1908. Davey Jones was on third base, with Schaefer on first, when Herman gave the sign that they should try for a double steal. However, when Herman took off for second base, catcher Nig Clarke just held on to the ball, forcing Jones to remain at third.

Schaefer looked over the situation and hollered, "Let's try it again!", and on the next pitch took off *back* towards first base, diving in with a head-first slide. This time the catcher was simply too dumbfounded to make a throw.

The umpires didn't know what to make of the play and allowed Schaefer to stay at first base—but he didn't hang around for long. On the next pitch, Schaefer gave a war whoop and again took off for second base. This time the catcher threw to second and Jones broke for the plate with both runners sliding in safely.

At first, it looked as if a daring new bit of strategy had been added to the game, and the only decision left was whether to credit Schaefer with three steals, two, or just one. It went into the record books as just one steal, and turned out to be one of a kind thanks to the reaction of the rulesmakers.

Despite the fact that Germany Schaefer's actions were strategically sound and actually helped the Tigers score a run, it was declared that such base running made a mockery of the game. The umpires were instructed to eject any future runners who attempted to steal backwards on the bases. This daring bit of base running began and ended with Herman "Germany" Schaefer, the man who stole first base.

Baseball's
Early Battles Against Smoking

With all the current fuss about smoking in the workplace and in public, one is reminded of the early days of this century when smoking was severely frowned upon, a situation that carried over into the baseball world.

At that time, two totally different attitudes were building toward the smoking of cigarettes. West of the Mississippi it was considered manly; but in the East, where all the major-league teams were located, it was considered depraved. In some circles it was actually considered effeminate. This created problems with those players who were raised in the West and believed smoking was perfectly normal. In 1907, manager Clark Griffith was so disgusted with the habit of his western imports that he openly banned cigarettes among his New York Highlanders.

This prejudice against smokers played a large role in the future of the Pittsburgh Pirates, whose owner, Barney Dreyfuss, was a firm believer that smoking was a sign of poor character. In one case, Dreyfuss refused to buy the contract of a young Texas player when he saw him smoking a cigarette on the bench. Dreyfuss proclaimed that "No man who smokes [cigarettes] will ever be a big league player." Well, that young player from Hubbard, Texas, turned out to be Hall of Famer Tris Speaker, who went on to hit .344 in a 22-year career.

Dreyfuss' prejudice denied the Pirates another Hall of Famer at about the same time. In 1906, Dreyfuss received a letter from a traveling salesman who was a loyal fan of the Pirates and wanted to report that he had come across a phenomenal pitching prospect. Dreyfuss refused to send someone to scout the lad, but not because he heard the boy was a smoker. No, the player was a clean-living farm boy who never smoked a cigarette in his life. Dreyfuss lost interest when he discovered that the traveling salesman sold cigars.

Because Dreyfuss refused to trust the judgment of a cigar salesman, the Pirates lost the services of one of the greatest pitchers of all time. The young pitcher from Humboldt, Kansas, who had impressed the cigar salesman was fireballer Walter Johnson.

The addition of Speaker and Johnson to the already talented Pirate team would have made them the dominant team of their era and perhaps of all time—but that was one dream that went up in smoke.

Lou Gehrig's
Consecutive Playing Streak

n May 31, 1925, Yankee shortstop Everett Scott saw his playing streak of 1,307 games come to an end. At the time, he was the only major leaguer to play in over 1,000 consecutive games. Sitting on the same bench was the rookie who would become the only player in baseball history to play more consecutive games than Scott.

In fact, Lou Gehrig began his streak the very next day by pinch-hitting for Pee Wee Wanninger, the shortstop who had replaced Scott to end his playing streak. The next day first baseman Wally Pipp, who had been beaned a few days

Lou Gehrig putting the tag on a fellow Yankee in spring training.

before, complained of a headache. Gehrig went into the starting lineup and stayed there for fourteen years.

In the end, Gehrig not only *broke* Scott's record, he *buried* it. He didn't beat it by ten or one hundred or even five hundred. Over five years after breaking Scott's record, the Iron Horse was still going strong out there every day. He finished at 2,130 games, which is more games than Scott played in his entire career! In fact, just the difference between Gehrig's streak and Scott's second-place streak would qualify as the ninth-longest playing streak in baseball history.

Gehrig's streak finally ended in 1939. By that time Lou was well out of the shadow of the retired Babe Ruth. Lou was regarded with affection in every ballpark in the land, and his record of playing in over 2,000 consecutive games had a special place in the consciousness of the fans.

What finally stopped the Iron Horse was the fatal amyotrophic lateral sclerosis, better known today as Lou Gehrig's disease. On May 2, 1939, the Yankees were in Detroit when Gehrig asked manager Joe McCarthy to take him out of the lineup. When the public address announcer called out the starting lineup and said, "Dahlgren, first base," the crowd was stunned into silence.

McCarthy had Gehrig take out the lineup card to the umpires and the crowd spontaneously rose for a standing ovation—a very rare tribute in those days.

On June 2, 1941, just a few weeks short of his thirty-eighth birthday, Lou Gehrig passed away. It was sixteen years to the day since Gehrig had replaced Wally Pipp in the Yankee lineup.

The Stories
Behind the Iron Horse

ost fans know that Lou Gehrig played fourteen years without missing a game before contracting a fatal disease in 1939, but few realize the pride Gehrig took in his playing streak and the things he endured to stay in the lineup every day.

There is no denying a bit of luck was involved. Gehrig never suffered a serious broken bone during the streak. Ironically, he did break a hand during an off-season tour of Japan and got a taste of the bench for the rest of the exhibition games. He didn't care much for the experience and went to great lengths to keep it from ever happening during the regular season.

Lou's major-league streak included several injuries that would have caused a lesser player to take a day or two off. The Iron Horse fractured a finger, suffered serious spike wounds, and was beaned three times in his career (including being knocked cold by one pitch), but he was always in there the next day.

Surprisingly, the greatest dangers to his streak came from muscle problems. Once he played with a charley horse so bad he could hardly walk, and occasionally he was plagued by bad back problems.

It was back trouble that nearly ended his streak in 1934. In *The Baseball Encyclopedia* there is an odd entry in Gehrig's record which shows that the left-handed thrower appeared in the lineup as a shortstop one time in 1934.

That's the summer Gehrig threw his back out and was forced to leave a game. The next day, Lou could hardly stand up. At that time Gehrig had already broken Everett Scott's record. There was nothing left for him to prove and, indeed, if he had stopped then he would still be baseball's Iron Man today. But Gehrig still wanted to play when he went to the ballpark.

The Yankees were on the road and manager Joe McCarthy decided to list Gehrig at shortstop and let him lead off the game. Then the regular shortstop would take over when the Yankees went out to the field. Although he was unable to stand up straight, Gehrig cut down his swing and stroked a solid single to right field before giving way to the pinch runner.

Gehrig healed quickly and won the Triple Crown that year. He also kept intact his playing streak, which would run for over 700 more games. With the drive Gehrig put into keeping his streak alive, it's almost as if he knew that the day he came out of the lineup would signal not only the end of his career but the end of his life.

The Greatest
Season That Almost Was

n September 11, 1922, George Sisler was sixteen games away from completing perhaps the greatest season in baseball history. He seemed a sure bet to set the all-time record for batting average. Hitting .400 was nothing new for Sisler, who had led the league with a .407 mark in 1920. Yet on this late date in the season, Sisler's average was up to an incredible .429, and he was on an incredible hot streak, hitting over .500 in his last one hundred at bats.

The famous first baseman had already collected 235 hits, and at his present pace would finish with a total of 262 hits. That would break the all-time record of 257 which Sisler had set in 1920. George was also just one game away from tying Ty Cobb's batting streak of forty games, which at that time was the longest in this century.

All three record-setting feats were endangered when Sisler seriously injured his right shoulder in a game against the Tigers. George sat out four days, but because his St. Louis Browns were in an intense pennant race with the Yankees, he returned to the lineup even though he had to lift his glove with both hands when there was a high throw at first. At the plate, Sisler had trouble hitting the higher pitches but still managed to go 1 for 4 and tie Cobb's record. The next day, he went 1 for 3 to break it. Then his luck ran out as he followed with an 0 for 4.

Because of the injury George didn't start seven of the last sixteen games, and when he was in there his batting average was off by over 100 points. He ended up missing the all-time hit record by twelve, and his batting average fell nine points to .420.

Sisler's batting streak of forty-one games was eventually surpassed by DiMaggio in 1941, and his .420 batting average fell to Rogers Hornsby who hit .424 in 1924.

George Sis

But Sisler still owns the highest batting average in the American League under modern conditions. When Nap Lajoie hit .422 in 1901, the league was using an old rule where foul balls were never counted as strikes.

Despite the injury, Sisler led the league in batting average, hits, runs, triples, and steals. He was named the 1922 Most Valuable Player, but the award was little comfort to Sisler, who was an ardent team player. With the exception of the 1944 wartime pennant, the Browns did not win a pennant in this century. The closest they came was the season in which their greatest player was injured with less than three weeks to go. The Yankees beat them by a single game.

Bill "Suitcase" Sisler

Bill Sisler is no relation to the baseball family of George Sisler, but perhaps he deserves a special niche in the Hall of Fame for his amazing desire to play professional baseball.

He started his baseball career with Elmira, New York, in 1923, and that began what appears to have been a tour of every minor league in the country. He rarely lasted a full season with any team, yet he never gave up his dream. He pursued his playing career for at least 25 years. In 1947, at age forty-three, he appeared in five different leagues, for six different clubs—and that's all in one season.

He was a slightly built left-hander who stood only five-feet-six. He was primarily a pitcher, but if a team needed an outfielder instead, he would try to talk his way into that position. The truth is, he was a horrible pitcher and probably a worse out-fielder. In twenty-five years, he won fewer than fifty games and had a winning percentage under .350.

It appears that Sisler would go from league to league searching for a team desperate for left-handed pitching. He'd talk his way onto the team and then quickly pitch his way off it. He averaged only seven pitching appearances per season. His twenty-five-year pretense as a minor-league ballplayer was so good that no one even knew what he was doing until his career was long over.

The National Association of Professional Baseball Leagues has a record of nearly every baseball contract in organized baseball since 1902. Recent research to deter-mine which player had signed the most professional contracts came up with a name that no one had ever heard of, the man known as "Suitcase" Sisler. No less than *fifty* different teams had a signed contract with Bill Sisler—and none ever asked him back the next year.

From 1923 to 1948, only the 1939 season lacked at least one contract signed by Sisler, and anyone who knows his story has to assume he was pitching that year under another name.

Efforts by baseball researchers to track down this quaint figure have been fruitless. They know he played and umpired semipro games in Rochester, New York, between his various minor-league stops, but no one knows where he is today. Appropriately, his last known address was around the corner from the minor-league park in Rochester. Our guess is that he's on a bus to Florida, where he'll talk his way onto a team of eighty-year-olds.

The 1953 Brooklyn Dodgers,
Baseball's Most Dominating Lineup

The 1953 Dodgers were the last team in baseball history to score 900 runs, and they did it with room to spare. They averaged 6.16 runs per game, pushing 955 runners across the plate. But their real claim to fame as baseball's most dominating offense is that no other National League team managed to score more than the 768 runs scored by the Cardinals and Giants.

That 187-run difference between first and second place erased the record of the 1931 Yankees as the top run-scoring team in baseball history. The Brooklyn club led the major leagues in batting average, slugging percentage, and on-base average.

The 1953 Brooklyn Dodgers, photographed just four games before clinching their second consecutive pennant.

They belted the most homers and stole the most bases. The league's batting champion, Carl Furillo, often hit seventh in the Dodgers' powerful lineup, and sometimes eighth.

Brooklyn's biggest advantage was behind the plate, where they had the league's Most Valuable Player in Roy Campanella. While the other starting catchers in the National League averaged only 9 homers and 38 RBIs, Roy slugged 41 homers and led the league with 142 RBIs.

The Brooklyn lineup gave an impressive demonstration of its explosiveness by setting an all-time record on May 24, 1953. The Dodgers came to bat in the eighth inning holding a slim 3-2 lead over the Phillies and finished the inning leading 16-2. Brooklyn scored thirteen runs in that inning without hitting a single home run and set two all-time records. One was for hitting two bases-loaded triples in the same inning, and the other was for scoring the most runs in an inning before a batter was retired.

The awesome Brooklyn lineup hit from top to bottom and halfway through again before recording their first out. The culprit was pitcher Carl Erskine, who had already singled earlier in the inning. (Who knows how far they would have gone if they had had a designated hitter!) In all, the Dodgers sent thirteen men to the plate and scored twelve runs before an out could be recorded. That broke a twenty-eight-year-old record, and it remains unmatched today, as does the dominance of that 1953 Dodger lineup.

Baseball's Strongest Throwing Arm

n baseball's early days, a popular promotion was a "Field Meet," which was a sort of Baseball Olympics in which players would compete to find out things like who was the fastest running around the bases and who could throw the ball the farthest.

The first 400-foot throw was recorded way back in 1872 when on October 15, Jim Hatfield of Cincinnati uncorked a throw of 400 feet, 7½ inches.

Forty-two years later, on October 9, 1910, Cincinnati again witnessed a legendary throw in a local field meet, this time by minor-league outfielder Larry LeJeune. The twenty-five-year-old right-hander launched a rocket of a throw that carried 425 feet, 9½ inches. It easily won the meet and was considered a throw that no one would ever top.

LeJeune became a minor celebrity in baseball circles and was signed shortly thereafter by the major-league Dodgers even though he was coming off a mediocre minor-league season. He ended up playing only 24 games in the majors and hit only .167 with just four RBIs, but when he passed away in 1952 at age 67, he still held the record as the only man to throw a baseball on the fly over 425 feet.

But less than five months after LeJeune's death, his 42-year-old record fell to another minor-league outfielder, Don "Buckeye" Grate. Don started his career as a pitcher and actually pitched briefly with the Phillies in 1943 and 1946. But Grate had control problems and eventually was shipped back to the minors where he was converted into an outfielder.

In 1952, at the annual Field Meet in Engel Stadium in Chattanooga, Tennessee, the twenty-nine-year-old right-hander stunned the crowd with a throw of 434 feet, 1 inch, breaking LeJeune's longstanding record by almost eight feet.

Surprisingly, Grate felt he still hadn't made his best throw. In the next year's field meet, on August 23, 1953, Buckeye Grate got it all in his fifth and final throw of the contest. When they stepped it off it came to 443 feet, 3½ inches. It was a new record by over nine feet, and even Buckeye conceded he couldn't throw a ball farther than that.

But where LeJeune's record lasted over forty years, Grate lost his title just four years later. In Omaha, on August 1, 1957, an American Association outfielder named Glen Gourbous set a new record with a throw measured at 455 feet, 3 inches. With the Field Meet becoming a thing of the past, Gourbous remains the king of the long-distance throwers.

Tom Zachary
and Babe Ruth

om Zachary was a left-hander who pitched for nineteen seasons in the majors from 1918 to 1936. He bounced around quite a bit, playing for seven teams, not counting a second tour with the Washington Senators. It was during his time with the Senators that Zachary first made a name for himself.

In 1924 the Washington club won their first pennant ever, and Zachary was the club's second-best pitcher behind Walter Johnson. Zachary went 15-9 and had the second-best ERA in the league. Then in the World Series, Zachary led the team to the World Championship by winning both his starts and allowing only two earned runs.

But over the years, baseball's memory of Tom Zachary has narrowed to the fact that he was the pitcher who surrendered Babe Ruth's sixtieth homer in 1927. There was nothing odd about Tom becoming Ruth's victim. Although the left-handed Zachary had the edge over Ruth, he was no stranger to Ruthian homers. In 1927 Babe hit a home run off Zachary nearly every time he faced him. Tom gave up home run number 22 in June, number 36 in August, and number 60 in September. Pouring further salt into the wound, all three of Babe's homers came with men on base.

But in 1929, Zachary found a positive niche in baseball's record book, and this time it came with the help of Ruth and the Yankees. It was a simple case of "If you can't beat 'em, join 'em." In August of 1928, less than a year after surrendering Ruth's sixtieth home run, Tom Zachary was traded to the Yankees. In 1929, working as a starter and reliever, he had his best year ever with the Babe hitting for him rather than against him.

That season Zachary turned in a career-low 2.48 ERA. He won three and lost none as a reliever, and he was a perfect 9-0 as a starter. His combined record of 12-0 went into the record books as an all-time record and remains the best single-season record for an undefeated pitcher in major-league history.

Tom Zachary in 1928.

Controversy Surrounding Joe DiMaggio's 56-Game Hitting Streak

A mong the few eyewitnesses to the entire fifty-six games of Joltin' Joe's legendary hitting streak, all will admit that a bit of luck was involved. The streak was kept alive by a single hit in better than 60 percent of the games. During the streak, DiMaggio hit only .408, which is just two points higher than Ted Williams hit for that entire season.

On at least four occasions, DiMaggio's lone hit was not sharply hit. Early in the streak, on May 30, DiMaggio's only hit for the day was a fly ball that got lost in the sun and fell at the feet of Boston outfielder Pete Fox. Three other times he kept the streak alive with infield hits.

On July 14, DiMaggio extended his streak to fifty-four games on a swinging bunt that traveled no more than forty feet. His two other infield hits were difficult calls for the official scorer. One was a sharply hit ball to the shortstop who was able to knock it down but was unable to make the throw. The other infield hit came in game 30 and some argue that this hit was really an error by the shortstop.

It happened on June 17 in Yankee Stadium in a game against the White Sox. DiMaggio was struggling to keep his streak alive and had managed to come up with just one hit in each of his previous three games. The opposing pitcher that day was right-hander Johnny Rigney of the White Sox—a pitcher who had always been tough on DiMaggio. Just a week before in Chicago, Rigney had nearly collared Joe when he held him to a single in five trips to the plate. In fact Rigney faced DiMaggio fifteen times during the streak and held Joe to four singles and a .267 average.

On June 17, Rigney had already retired Joe three times when he hit what appeared to be a routine grounder to shortstop Luke Appling. The ball surprised Appling by taking a high hop up to his chest and caroming off his shoulder into left field. Several observers felt that Appling had misplayed the hop and, at worst, could have blocked the ball and made the throw.

The official scorer was a reporter named Dan Daniel, and he recorded it as a bad-hop single. At that time scoring decisions were not routinely announced to the crowd, and many fans left the park believing it had been an error and that DiMaggio's streak was over.

It is possible that Daniel's scoring of the play was not totally objective. Daniel was an ardent admirer of DiMaggio's play; Joe was his favorite Yankee player and Daniel considered him a friend. In fact, Daniel once wrote a column titled "My Friend—The Yankee Clipper."

Did DiMaggio really collect legitimate hits in fifty-six consecutive games? That was the question in 1941, and without the luxury of a film record, it remains a question that may never be answered.

DiMaggio's Handicap in his 56-Game Hitting Streak

There are always obstacles to keeping any hitting streak alive, but Joe DiMaggio faced a special problem during his legendary hitting streak of 1941.

Like most ballplayers, Joe DiMaggio was very attached to his bats, and he was particularly pleased with a bat he began using early in 1941. It was a D-29 model weighing thirty-six ounces, just like the rest of his bats, but it had a special feel to DiMaggio. It was a durable bat, and Joe had used it all season through June 29.

That day he was playing in a doubleheader against the Senators. In the first game he smacked a double to run his hitting streak to forty-one games. But when

DiMaggio fouls one off during the streak.

DiMaggio came back out for the second game, his favorite bat was missing. It appeared that a fan had raided the Yankee bat rack during the doubleheader intermission and stolen Joe's bat as a souvenir.

DiMaggio was devastated by the loss. Tommy Henrich, the Yankee right fielder, offered Joe the use of his bat, which was also a D-29 model. Henrich claimed it was an especially good bat, but DiMaggio didn't want to use another player's bat and made three straight outs using his own backup bats.

When Joe came up in the seventh inning still hitless, Tommy Henrich again urged him to borrow his D-29 bat. Finally Joe agreed to try it, and lined a single to extend the streak to forty-two games. When DiMaggio broke Wee Willie Keeler's record hitting streak of forty-four games with a home run off Dick Newsome, he was still using Henrich's bat, but he had not stopped trying to get back his lucky bat.

Fortunately, the bat thief began to feel the pangs of conscience and sent word that he wanted to return the bat if he could do so anonymously. DiMaggio quickly agreed and had his old bat in hand for the final eleven games of the streak. His first hit with the old bat was a home run, and in the next ten games he hit .575, including two four-hit games. It was the hardest he had hit the ball during the entire streak.

Even when the streak ended, DiMaggio felt he had hit the ball as hard as ever, but right at the fielders. Joe went on to hit in another seventeen straight games with the wonderful piece of wood that was so much a part of his streak.

King of the B.P. Pitchers

aseball fans are always interested in the best at this or that—best lefty hitter, best right-handed pitcher, best pinch hitter, best strikeout pitcher—but has anyone ever wondered who was baseball's greatest batting-practice pitcher?

Back before World War II, throwing B.P. was a serious chore that could decide whether a borderline pitcher rode the trains in the majors or the buses in the minors. Most teams did not have a large enough, or young enough, coaching staff to throw regular batting practice. In the spring, when the time came to choose the last pitcher, the nod often went to the guy with the rubber arm who could throw batting practice day after day.

The master of this unique art was Henry Grampp, a minor-league pitcher the Chicago Cubs picked up in 1927. Hall of Fame manager Joe McCarthy was first to recognize Grampp's rare value. The twenty-three-year-old right-hander had all the pitches, but none were outstanding and his fastball was below average. But young Hank was ambidextrous and liked to fool around throwing left-handed on the sidelines. McCarthy immediately envisioned Grampp as the ideal batting-practice pitcher. By switching arms, he could be more durable—and he could prepare the Cubs for both left- and right-handed pitching.

Grampp took his role with the Cubs very seriously. He studied the various pitchers around the league so he could duplicate their mannerisms in batting practice when they were the Cubs' opponents. Grampp rarely got in a game but remained with the Cubs through their pennant winning season of 1929.

Hank was eligible to pitch during the regular season, and the Chicago Cubs were forced to use him in relief a couple of times in 1927. He struck out three batters in three innings, but he gave up four hits and three runs for a 9.00 ERA. His next major-league appearance did not come until late in 1929 after the Cubs had already clinched the pennant. The Cubs rewarded Grampp with his first and only major-league start. Hank lasted only two innings and allowed six runs to take the loss and raise his career ERA to 16.20.

Habits are hard to break. The man who could make Carl Hubbell, Burleigh Grimes, and Dazzy Vance hittable in batting practice had made Hank Grampp hittable, too.

The Minor-League Home Run King

Although he never played a day in the major leagues, many baseball fans recognize the name of Joe Bauman as the legendary Babe Ruth of the minors.

Joe was a big old boy out of Welch, Oklahoma. The first baseman stood all of six-feet-five and weighed 235 pounds. His early career in professional baseball was spotty and included only 427 professional games before age thirty. He retired once at age nineteen, served three years in World War II, and retired again for three years at age twenty-six.

But Bauman was all business when he returned to baseball at age thirty-one. Playing for Artesia and Roswell in the Longhorn League, he took three straight

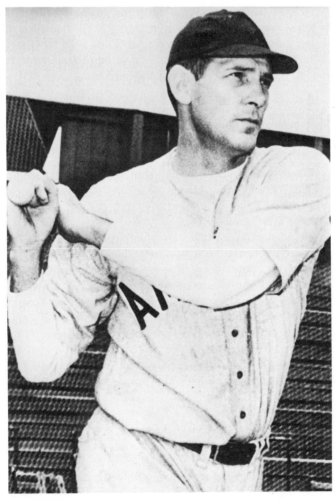

Joe Bauman

home run crowns with fifty homers or more. In 1954, he set the all-time minor-league record by belting seventy-two homers. What makes the record even more impressive is that he did it in only 498 at bats, better than a home run every seven at bats.

The frequency of Bauman's home runs was remarkable throughout his career. He averaged fifty homers for every 150 games played, and for the last five seasons of his career he averaged a homer every 8.6 at bats. That's better than Babe Ruth's best single season mark.

Joe was not just a home run hitter. His minor-league career average was .337, and the year he hit his seventy-two homers he also took the batting title with an even .400 average. In fact, it was the most dominating Triple Crown performance ever, as the left-handed slugger also had 224 RBIs in just 138 games.

Yet, because of his late start, Bauman was never considered a serious major-league prospect. Less than two years after his record-setting season, Bauman retired for good, even though he was just thirty-four years old and still belting out a homer every ten at bats. He finished with a remarkable 337 homers in barely seven full seasons and more RBIs than games played (1,057 RBIs in 1,019 games). His combination of power and batting average made him the only player in professional baseball to retire with a career slugging percentage over .700.

Mr. E-6

There really are no poor-fielding shortstops who make it to the major leagues, certainly not among those who play over 600 games at the position. But some are more exasperating than others. Consider that old Chicago Cub, Lennie Merullo.

Lennie played his whole career with the Cubs from 1941 to 1947. He had decent range in the field and occasionally made the spectacular play, but he was famous for booting a phenomenal number of routine chances.

Year after year, Merullo made a ton of errors. In the four seasons during which he played one hundred games at shortstop he always had the lowest or next-to-lowest fielding average in the league, and his fielding average consistently came in under .950. How bad is that? Well, Dick Groat set a major-league record by leading the league in errors six times and still fielded .962 in his career.

Still, Merullo was the Cubs' starting shortstop in 1945 when they won the pennant. Of course, they didn't have a lot of choices as their only alternative in that war year was a gimpy thirty-four-year-old second baseman named Roy Hughes. And Hughes might have beat Merullo out if he hadn't been disabled by a knee injury for much of the year. As it was, Merullo fielded .948, and when Hughes came off the disabled list at the end of the season, he took over as the Cubs' shortstop in the World Series.

After the war, when Hughes was traded to Philadelphia, Merullo lost the short-stop job to Billy Jurges, who was returning to big-league action at age thirty-eight. Then, in 1947, Jurges became a player-coach and the thirty-year-old Merullo was given his last chance to show he was steady enough in the field to hold down the shortstop position. Lennie booted away his career as he led the league in errors, an especially difficult feat as Merullo played in only 108 games. Lennie's fielding percentage was the lowest among National League shortstops by almost twenty points, and he never played another game in the majors.

A clue that Merullo was going to be unusually error-prone could be found way back in 1942, Lennie's first full season in the majors. On a Sunday afternoon, September 13, Lennie made four errors at shortstop. *In one inning.*

Yes, right there in the second inning, Merullo put himself firmly into the record books. He tied a National League record which had stood for over fifty years, since a rookie shortstop named Shorty Fuller, playing for the Washington Nationals, had made four errors in an inning in 1888. Of course Shorty was playing with some handicaps like an all-dirt infield and probably a lopsided ball. Heck, in that period it's possible that Shorty wasn't even wearing a glove. Maybe Merullo should have tried that. In that inning it couldn't have hurt.

The Defense of the DiMaggios

W hen fans refer to Joe DiMaggio as Joe D., they often add that the "D" stands for defense. In that sense there was also a Dom D. and a Vince D. All three of the DiMaggio brothers were outstanding defensive center fielders. Dominic and Vincent clearly did not have the power of their superstar brother, but the truth is that both assembled better defensive records in the major leagues than their brother Joe. Consider the evidence. Which of the DiMaggio brothers was placed in center field in his rookie season? That was Vince with the Boston Braves. Dom was the Red Sox right fielder in his rookie year, and Joe was stationed in left field as a rookie Yankee.

The three DiMaggios: Vince, Joe, and Dom.

Which DiMaggio had the most seasons with four hundred or more outfield putouts? Dominic held the American League record with four such seasons until Chet Lemon bumped him in 1985. Joe did it three times and Vince did it twice—which was pretty good as Vincent had only five seasons during which he played more than 130 games (Joe had ten and Dom had eight).

Which DiMaggio is one of only five outfielders who has caught five hundred flyballs in a season? That's Dominic with 503 in 1948. Vince's best was 457, and Joe's was 441.

Which brother never led his league in errors? That's Vince. Dom did it one year with ten. Joe did it with seventeen.

Which DiMaggio led his league in outfield assists the most times? Dominic led three times, Vince did it twice, and Joe, only once.

Which brother led most often in outfield double plays? Both Dom and Vincent did it twice; Joe did it once.

A comparison of their career defensive records shows a similar pattern, with Joe having trouble keeping up with brothers Dom and Vince.

Per 150 Outfield Games in the Major Leagues					
	Put-Outs	Assists	Errors	DPs	Fielding %
Dominic	422	16.1	9.7	3.5	.9783
Vincent	397	17.7	8.0	4.8	.9811
Joseph	394	13.3	9.2	2.6	.9780

In the key category of most putouts per outfield game, it's the youngest brother Dominic out front, Vince second, and Joe third. The only category that Joe isn't last in is average of total errors, but Dominic handled so many extra chances that his fielding percentage was actually slightly higher than Joe's. In fact, in outfield assists, double plays, and fielding percentage, the order is consistent: Vince, Dom, and Joe.

It appears Vincent had the strongest arm, Dominic the most range, and Joe—well, he was a great defensive outfielder, but without the bat he was nothing special in the DiMaggio family.

The Day
the Fans Took Over the Ballpark

On April 11, 1912, Opening Day in Brooklyn, the Dodgers played host to their arch rivals the New York Giants. The Dodgers were playing their last season in Washington Park, a small wooden structure that was designed to seat only 18,000 fans. The game was a sellout and management was selling standing-room-only tickets, but thousands of frustrated fans filled the streets.

One group of fans stormed the left-field wall and a whole section of the wall collapsed under their weight. Soon the ballpark was filled with thousands of spectators who had bypassed the price of admission. One report claimed there were at least 7,000 fans on the field itself, and they actively resisted efforts to push them back.

Hoodlums stole the chairs from the box-seat areas and stood on them to further block the view of those in the stands. The players had no room to warm up on the sidelines. Then they discovered the crowd had confiscated their benches, forcing the players to sit on the ground.

When the Mayor threw out the first ball he couldn't even see the diamond. He threw the ball in the general direction of home plate, where a fan grabbed it and very considerately handed it to the catcher. The only people who could actually see the contest were the fans ringing the infield or standing on chairs or benches. Two fans climbed the wire backstop and relayed the plays down to the sportswriters who were totally screened off from the action.

Fearing the crowd might turn angry if the game were canceled, the Giants and Dodgers agreed to go ahead and play. The crowd stepped back from the infield to allow the contest to proceed, and a ground rule was established that a ball hit into the thickest parts of the outfield crowd would go as a double.

As the thick crowd crept closer to the infield, the game turned into a bizarre contest to see which team could loft the most balls into the outfield. The game featured seventeen ground-rule doubles, thirteen by the Giants, who won the game 18-3.

After six innings, homeplate umpire Bill Klem suddenly called the game because of darkness. The sun was still well above the horizon, but it was a merciful ending to a baseball travesty.

Professional Baseball's RBI King

I n recent years, there has been renewed interest in documenting top minor-league performances. When researchers began searching for the best RBI performance in a professional season, they first turned to the early days of the Pacific Coast League. Back in the 1920s, teams played extended schedules that included as many as 220 games a season.

They discovered the RBI record-holder in the West Texas-New Mexico League, which played a normal minor-league schedule of 140 games back in 1948. It definitely was an offensive league, though, as it produced three .400 hitters, and the number two man in RBIs had an astounding total of 196, the seventh-highest total in baseball history.

But no one was close to the RBI leader, Big Bob Crues. Bob was a former pitcher who once won twenty games in the same league. He hurt his arm, and when he returned from serving two years in the military during World War II, he became an outfielder at age twenty-six. Because of the late start as a hitter, Crues was never considered a serious major-league prospect, but his amazing 1948 season will keep his name alive in baseball's memory.

In 1948, at age twenty-nine, Big Bob was in the prime of his life. The star hitter for

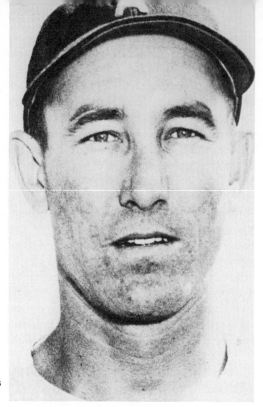

Bob Crues

Amarillo stood six-feet-three, weighed 190 pounds, swung the bat right-handed, and—as befits a man who would set a Ruthian record—played right field.

Crues played every one of the team's 140 games, hit .404 and led the league with 185 runs scored. His sixty-nine homers led the league easily and his slugging percentage was around .850.

As impressive as that sounds, other minor leaguers had put up similar numbers before. Minor-league legend Joe Bauman once hit .400 with seventy-two homers. But no one has come close to Crues's record for driving runners home. Big Bob set one all-time professional record by belting *eight* grand slams that season. When the last runner had come home, the league statistics showed that Bob Crues had knocked home *254* runs!

The magnitude of this accomplishment is difficult to comprehend. The difference between the first- and second-highest RBI totals in the major leagues is only six RBIs (Wilson's 190 and Gehrig's 184). The difference between the second- and third-highest totals in the minors is only two (Bauman's 224 and Tony Lazzeri's 222). But the difference between Crues' 254 RBIs and those of any other professional ballplayer is no less than 30!

At total of 254 RBIs in one season seemed unthinkable in the context of Crues's own career. Just two years earlier he had hit .341 with twenty-nine home runs, which was good for 120 RBIs. Crues better than *doubled* that total in 1948. The next year Crues hit "only" twenty-nine homers with 129 RBIs. He never had another season like that magnificent summer of 1948.

Babe Ruth's Home Run Firsts

abe hit only one home run in his brief minor-league stay, but his first home run as a professional player came months earlier while in spring training with his minor-league club, the Baltimore Orioles.

It was Saturday, March 7, 1914, Babe's debut as a professional player. It was only an exhibition game, and a loose one at that. Ruth pitched and also played some at shortstop despite being a left-handed thrower. In Ruth's second at bat, the nineteen-year-old, moon-faced rookie swung from the heels and blasted the ball into a distant cornfield beyond right field. A few years earlier, the legendary athlete Jim Thorpe had hit the longest homer ever seen at that field. The spectators estimated that Ruth had slugged the ball sixty feet farther than Thorpe's memorable blast!

Hungry for baseball news, the Baltimore papers featured Ruth's home run in headlines that would be repeated many times in the future. They read "HOMER BY RUTH FEATURE OF GAME" and "RUTH MAKES MIGHTY CLOUT." The newspaper account of the blow said, "The next batter made a hit that will live in the memory of all who saw it. That clouter was George Ruth, the southpaw from St. Mary's School. The ball carried so far to right field that he walked around the bases."

A little more than a year later Ruth hit his first major-league home run. On May 6, pitcher Jack "The Crab" Warhop became the first of many victims as Ruth connected in only the eighteenth at bat of his young career.

There were several ironic touches to home run number one in a string of 714. The home run was hit in the Polo Grounds—the park that five years later would be Babe's home field. There, in 1920, he would usher in the live-ball era by hitting fifty-four homers, nearly doubling his own single-season record of twenty-nine in 1919.

Adding to the irony is the fact that Warhop was pitching for the New York Highlanders, the team that became the Yankees—the team with which Ruth was destined to make home run history.

The Babe's Greatest Season...as a Pitcher

efore Ruth was converted to the outfield, he was one of the best left-handed pitchers in baseball. Ruth always took a special pride in this side of his magnificent baseball skills. When asked for the personal favorite of his many baseball feats, Babe once surprised his listeners by citing a game in which he loaded the bases and then struck out Detroit's three best batters: Ty Cobb, Sam Crawford, and Bobbie Veach.

1916 was easily the Babe's best season on the mound. Although he was only twenty-two and the youngest pitcher on Boston's staff, Ruth was chosen to open the season and responded with a 2-1 victory. The Red Sox battled for the pennant all year long and Ruth pitched one key victory after another. In late July he put Boston into first place with a 6-0 shutout. In mid-August he beat Walter Johnson 1-0 in thirteen innings, and then in his next start blanked second-place Detroit 3-0.

In September Ruth beat Walter Johnson again, this time 2-1 to give him his fifth straight victory over the Big Train! Walter ended that year by winning two more games than Ruth, but Babe's twenty-three victories led all left-handers, and it was Ruth who led the league in ERA with a mark of 1.75. Babe also led the league by allowing only 6.4 hits per nine innings; he was second in winning percentage, and third in both innings and strikeouts. Ruth also led the league in shutouts with nine, including two in his final starts of the season. Over eighty years later, that remains the American League record for left-handers.

Babe Ruth with the Red Sox in 1915.

The Babe was in great form as Boston beat Brooklyn four games to one in the World Series. Ruth pitched brilliantly in the crucial second game. With the Dodgers seeking to tie the Series at one game apiece, Ruth took a 1-1 tie into extra innings and refused to give in. He allowed only six hits as he won 2-1 in fourteen innings, the longest game in World Series history.

The lone run against Ruth came in the first inning. The following thirteen shutout innings became a streak of twenty-two shutout innings in 1918 when he won another thriller, 1-0, to open that year's World Series. In his third and final appearance as a World Series pitcher, Ruth won 3-2 but did not surrender a run until the seventh inning. That gave Ruth a streak of 29⅔ consecutive shutout innings in World Series competition. This broke a highly celebrated record of Christy Mathewson's and remained the record for forty-two years till broken by Whitey Ford in 1961.

When Ruth was dying in 1948, he held over seventy-five baseball records but he still cited his World Series shutout string among his proudest accomplishments.

Baseball's
Most Daring Traders

F rank "Trader" Lane was always good copy during the winter "hot stove" league because he was always in the middle of lively trade rumors. But no rumors could match the actual excitement of the deals engineered when Lane hooked up with trading partner Bill DeWitt in 1960. At that time Lane was Cleveland's general manager and DeWitt was president of the Detroit Tigers.

It is Lane who takes credit for suggesting a trade of star outfielder Rocky Colavito for the Tigers' star outfielder Harvey Kuenn. What made the offer so intriguing was that in 1959 Colavito had hit 42 homers to take the home run crown and Kuenn had hit .353 to take the batting championship. DeWitt said, "Sure, why not?", and they pumped the deal for all the drama they could by holding back the announcement until the day before the season opener. It remains the only time in baseball history that the batting champion has been traded for the home run king.

Detroit got the best of the Colavito-Kuenn deal. The Rock led the Tigers in home runs and RBIs while Kuenn's average fell 45 points and he drove in only 54 runs. But that didn't discourage Cleveland's Trader Lane. As the Tigers and Indians went into the last third of the 1960 season, neither DeWitt nor Lane was satisfied with his field manager. So, the two executives did what any two trading fools would do, *they traded managers.* The Tigers sent manager Jimmy Dykes to Cleveland for Indians manager Joe Gordon.

This time there was no winner in their unusual transaction. Both managers had worse records with their new clubs than with the old ones. But DeWitt got the edge again as the Tigers were hurt slightly less and gained a game on the Indians after the trade.

Oddly enough, it was Bill DeWitt of the Tigers who was asked to step down after the 1960 season. A little thing like getting fired wasn't going to stop DeWitt from trading until he got it right. He immediately became the general manager of the Cincinnati Reds and engineered a series of brilliant trades that turned the sub-.500 franchise into the 1961 champions of the National League.

Baseball's
Most Eccentric Player

When Bill Veeck owned the minor-league franchise in Milwaukee, he had a shortstop named Jackie Price who practiced harder than anybody. The only problem was, the things Jackie practiced were not going to win any ballgames.

For example, Price learned to catch and throw a baseball while standing on his head. He then learned to throw left-handed until he could throw both a curve and a fastball—one lefty, one righty—*at the same time*. Price was so blasé about his unusual skills that he claimed the toughest part of the trick was finding two catchers to practice with.

Jackie Price in a typical batting stance.

When Price got bored with that, he practiced his hitting while hanging upside down from a trapeze. He learned to hit a ball while swinging the bat behind his back, and he became an enemy of the groundskeeper who one day discovered Price shagging flies while driving a jeep in the outfield. The groundskeeper wasn't impressed that Jackie was also catching the balls behind his back.

Although Price was an entertainer with the diamond as his stage, he was still a ballplayer and he got his chance to play in the majors as Lou Boudreau's back-up shortstop in 1946. Unfortunately, another of Jackie's eccentricities sent him back to the minors. You see, Jackie also had a fondness for snakes and actually took his favorite pet on road trips with him.

After taking that small liberty, it wasn't long before Price began wearing a *live* snakeskin belt outside his hotel room. One one road trip he thought it would be funny to release his snake in a railroad dining car loaded with women. The effect was predictable, and when an angry conductor asked Jackie who he thought he was, Price, was incapable, as usual, of giving a straight answer. He said he was Lou Boudreau, manager of the Indians.

The real Boudreau was not amused when train officials showed up at his compartment determined to throw him off at the next stop. The gag was especially unfunny coming from a backup shortstop hitting .231.

That was the end of Jackie Price's major-league career, but he did go on to become a one-man show of baseball tricks never seen before or since.

Baseball's
Third Major League

uring the nineteenth century there were several different leagues that the record books recognize as major, but in this century there have been only three major leagues: the American, the National, and the short-lived Federal League. The Federal league was brought into existence in 1914 and was backed by a group of newly rich industrialists. They placed franchises in established major-league cities like Brooklyn, Chicago, St. Louis, and Pittsburgh, but they also opened new territory in Kansas City, Indianapolis, Baltimore, and Buffalo. In 1915 they closed the Indianapolis franchise and brought major-league baseball to Newark, New Jersey.

The Federal League's choices in team nicknames were rather odd. They had the Brooklyn "Tip-Tops," which made a certain sense as the club's owner also owned the Tip-Top Bakery. Their Baltimore club was known as the Terrapins after the freshwater turtle, and actually had a turtle emblem on their uniforms. Probably the oddest nickname was used in Chicago. If you were in a city a thousand miles from the nearest ocean and were trying to promote a game of athletic skill and grace, would you dub your team the Chicago Whales?

The Federalists gained major-league status by openly raiding the rosters of the two established leagues, which led to bidding wars that threatened the stability of all three leagues. In the end, 172 players with American or National League experience signed Federal League contracts. Their rosters included Hall of Famers Eddie Plank, Three-Finger Brown, Chief Bender, Joe Tinker, and Ed Roush.

Unfortunately, the Federal League was underfinanced and shortly succumbed to monetary and legal problems. When peace talks began with the established leagues in 1915, it was decided that two of the Federal League owners could purchase the two established franchises that were up for sale, the Chicago Cubs and the St. Louis Browns. The Federal League player contracts were all auctioned off to the highest bidder.

The only remnant of the Federal League is a ballpark in Chicago. Wrigley Field, the home of the Chicago Cubs, was originally known as Weeghman Park, taking its name from Charlie Weeghman, a wealthy restaurant-chain owner who also owned the Chicago Whales in the Federal League. Weeghman built the park strictly for them, and they were the park's only tenants until the league folded and the Cubs took it over in 1916.

Benny Kauff,
Star of the Federal League

n 1914 and 1915, baseball's short-lived Federal League had to base its popularity on star players it stole from the established leagues. As luck would have it, the league also quickly developed its own star player in Benny Kauff, a young outfielder with tremendous speed.

Kauff actually had received a five-game trial with the Yankees in 1912, but in 1914 the twenty-four-year-old lefty seemed to come out of nowhere to dominate the new major league. That first season he played right field for the pennant-winning Indianapolis club. He led the league in total hits and doubles and took the batting title with a .370 average. They called him "The Federal League Ty Cobb" as he also stole seventy-five bases, twenty-eight more than anyone else in the league.

The next year he ended up with the Brooklyn Tip-Tops, and again took the Federal League batting title, this time with a .342 average. He also was the league's leading slugger and once more led the league with fifty steals. Kauff enjoyed his newfound stardom and took to the high life. His teammates remember him showing off his diamond rings and wearing silk underwear to the ballpark.

When the Federal League folded, the clubs were forced to sell their players to the highest bidder. Benny Kauff naturally had the highest price tag and the New York Giants paid a staggering $35,000 for the young star who was still only twenty-six years old.

At first, Kauff seemed overmatched by the National League. In 1916 he was second in the league with forty steals, but he hit only .264. But the next year he helped the Giants win the pennant with a .308 batting average that led the club and was also fourth best in the league. In 1918 he got off to a good start, hitting .315, but

Benny Kauff, the "Federal
League Ty Cobb."

in mid-season he decided to enlist in the military and serve in World War I.

Back with the Giants in 1919, he hit only .277 and his career ended suddenly the next year at age thirty. Kauff's taste for the good life was his downfall. Benny was always short of funds, and one story suggests he entered the military in 1918 simply to avoid paying some of his considerable debts.

In 1919, Kauff was linked to several shady dealings, including the possible fixing of baseball games (possibly even the 1919 World Series!). In 1920, he was charged with car theft and receiving stolen goods. Even though Kauff was acquitted of these charges, baseball commissioner Landis banned him from baseball.

In the game of life, Benny Kauff—the star of the Federal League, two-time batting champion, and career .311 hitter—had struck out.

The Umpire's Nightmare

It's possible to have an extra ball that escapes from the bullpen or is thrown from the stands onto the playing field. Officially, however, there can be only one ball in play, and that is the ball put into play by the umpire. But what happens when the umpire puts two balls into play?

It actually happened on June 30, 1959, in a game between the Cardinals and the Cubs. It began when Chicago's Bob Anderson threw a 3-1 pitch inside to Stan Musial that got past catcher Sammy Taylor and went all the way back to the screen.

Umpire Vic Delmore called it ball four and Taylor started arguing that the ball had nicked Musial's bat and should be a foul. Third baseman Alvin Dark ended up having to race to the backstop to get the ball from the batboy who thought it was a foul because the catcher hadn't chased it. In an attempt to take advantage of the confusion, first-base coach Harry Walker waved Musial around first and on to second.

Back at home plate, umpire Delmore tried to signal an end to Taylor's argument by slamming a new baseball in his glove and telling him to play ball. What he had forgotten is that time had not been called and they were actually in the middle of a play. Dark retrieved the original ball at the screen and made a low throw that shortstop Ernie Banks came up with while Musial was sliding into second base.

When pitcher Bob Anderson saw Musial taking off for second base, he grabbed the second ball out of Taylor's glove and threw it to second base.

Having caught one ball already, Banks showed no interest in catching Anderson's throw, which sailed past him into the outfield. When Musial saw that ball bouncing into center field, he got up and took off for third base, whereupon Banks said. "Look what I've got, Stan," and tagged out the flabbergasted Musial.

How did the umpire settle this one? There was no help from the rulebook in this case. After considerable confusion and debate, the umpires decided that the original ball had to be considered the ball in play. That's the ball Stan Musial was tagged with, so Stan was out. Fortunately, the Cardinals went on to win the game, overcoming umpire Delmore's mistake in putting a second ball into play. And the umpire's decision stands as the precedent should this umpire's nightmare ever happen again.

The Ugliest No-Hitter in History

ost no-hitters are crisp pitching performances of rare beauty, but with over 200 major-league no-hitters on the books, there are bound to be a few clunkers. Howard Ehmke's 1923 whitewash leads the way in this exotic category.

To begin with, Ehmke's opponents on that fateful September 7 were not exactly the 1927 Yankees. The 1923 Philadelphia Athletics were a rag-tag outfit that scored fewer runs than any team other than Ehmke's own last-place Red Sox. The Athletics had already suffered a no-hitter just three days earlier at the hand of Sam Jones of the Yankees.

Howard Ehmke

Still, Ehmke needed a little luck right from the start. Leadoff batter Wid Matthews hit Ehmke's first pitch on a line drive right up the middle, but Howard managed to tip it with his glove just enough to deflect it to his shortstop.

In the second inning, another line drive was ripped up the middle. Ehmke wanted no part of this one, but while he tried to dodge the ball, it lodged in his glove which was, according to the *Philadelphia Ledger*, "...sticking out behind him." The Athletics continued to make easy contact with Ehmke's pitches. Howard did not retire a single batter on a swinging strike three, and only one went down looking at a final strike.

But all of this was nothing compared to the events that preserved Ehmke's no-hitter in the later innings. With two outs in the sixth inning, Howard Ehmke was a good bet to extend his no-hitter into the seventh. Standing at the plate was Slim Harris, the opposing pitcher and a horrible hitter who carried a batting average of .066.

Yet Harris cracked a line drive that cleared the shortstop's head and split the outfielders for an apparent double. Ah, but the Red Sox appealed that Harris had missed first base. The umpire agreed, and what looked like a perfectly clean hit went into the boxscore as an out!

Then, in the eighth inning, with the crowd asking themselves how this could still be a no-hitter, Ehmke's left fielder dropped a low line drive at his knees. Howard's luck held out as the official scorer first ruled it a hit but quickly changed his mind and made it an error. Ehmke went on to retire the side in the ninth—and walked away with the lone no-hitter of his career.

A Near Miss at Baseball's First Consecutive No-Hitters

n September 11, 1923, the final out of the game between the Red Sox and Yankees set off a tremendous cheer in Yankee Stadium, even though the Yankees had lost. The 15,000 fans believed they were cheering the first pitcher ever to hurl consecutive no-hitters.

No, they weren't cheering Johnny Vander Meer, who was only eight years old in 1923; they were cheering Boston pitcher Howard Ehmke who was accepting congratulations for throwing a no-hitter after he had blanked the Athletics in the hit column just four days earlier.

In those days, the ballpark scoreboard gave only the run total and there was no public address system. What Ehmke and the crowd didn't know was that an apparent error in the first inning had been scored as a hit.

It is not unheard of for an official scorer to change a call after a game is completed, and three no-hitters have gone into the books when the official scorer changed a hit to an error after the game was over (Jeff Tesreau in 1912, Ernie Koob in 1917, and Virgil Trucks in 1952 were the lucky pitchers). But the official scorer at this game was Fred Leib, and he had a firm policy of standing by his original decisions, just as an umpire sometimes had to stand by a bad call. In this case, Leib had more than a little reason to believe he had muffed his call.

How bad a decision was it? The controversial first-inning hit was awarded to the Yankees' speedy leadoff batter, Whitey Witt. It was a chopper to third baseman Howard Shanks, a steady fielder who had led the league in fielding percentage back in 1921. But Shanks bobbled this ball against his chest and didn't even attempt a throw. Leib felt it took a strange hop which kept the fielder from having a shot at throwing out the fleet-footed Witt. But even Leib described it as a "doubtful call" that could have gone either way.

However, most key observers and the majority of the crowd had assumed it was an error. Retired Hall of Fame shortstop Joe Tinker was sitting in a third-base box seat, right on top of the play, and called it "definitely an error." The home plate umpire was Hall of Famer Tom Connally, and he said, "If that wasn't an error, I never saw one."

Surprisingly, Ehmke took the bad news stoically. He knew his first no-hitter had been tainted by an apparent double that was nullified when the batter missed first base. He had thrown a no-hitter that should have been a one-hitter; it seemed only fair that he now threw a one-hitter that was really a no-hitter.

What goes around comes around—it just happened awfully fast this time.

The Superstitious Superstar

Ty Cobb was not the kind of player one would expect to have a strong superstitious streak. He was known as a smart player who took a scientific approach to his conditioning and his play. In spring training he wore shoe insoles made of lead to strengthen his legs for the regular season, and he began the practice of swinging the weight of several bats while in the on-deck circle. In his private life he was a shrewd, practical businessman who became a millionaire many times over.

Yet Cobb, like many ballplayers, was deeply superstitious. He was a fanatic believer in trying to do things exactly the same when he was in a hot hitting streak. He would have the same breakfast, take the same route to the ballpark, hang his shower towel on the same hook and—perhaps taking it a bit too far—he refused to allow his uniform to be cleaned.

As one opposing pitcher noted, you could tell if Cobb was having one of his hot streaks by how bedraggled and dirty his uniform was. Given Ty's career average of .367 and a number of lengthy batting streaks—including one that reached forty games—Cobb's teammates would probably have preferred to do without that superstition.

Cobb's strongest superstition involved what he believed was a magic bat. His talent seemed to explode in his third season, 1907. At that point, Ty had never led the league in any category, but suddenly he found himself leading the Tigers to the pennant and dominating the league with 212 hits, 116 RBIs and forty-nine steals. He easily took the batting title with a .350 average and also led the league in slugging percentage.

During the season Cobb had begun using a black bat and he became convinced that it had magical properties. Ty was also afraid that if he broke the bat, it would lose its magic. So after the 1907 season he never used the bat in a game again. Cobb continued to take his magic bat to all his games and would swing it along with his game bat in the on-deck circle.

Cobb's special regard for this bat can be seen in a photo from his 1908 wedding. At the cake-cutting ceremony there is only one baseball artifact in the picture. The hand of Ty Cobb rests on his black 1907 championship bat.

Ty Cobb

Ty Cobb
of the Cleveland Indians?

n 1906, Ty Cobb was nineteen years old and beginning to show his promise as a master batsman. He appeared in just 98 games, but by the end of the season had clearly beaten out Davey Jones for the Tigers' center field job, outhitting Jones by sixty points, .320 to .260. If Ty had qualified for the batting title, his .320 average would have ranked him fourth in the league.

Yet Detroit was not convinced that keeping Cobb was in their best interest. Club owner Frank Navin knew that Ty had been at the center of all the bickering on the Tiger club, which had a losing record in 1906. The young rebel from Georgia had gotten into a number of fights with his teammates, and new manager Hughie Jennings was having some trouble with Cobb in spring training.

In the spring of 1907, Cleveland president Charles Sommers got a call from the Tigers, offering to trade Cobb for center fielder Elmer Flick. Now Flick was a pretty good player. He eventually was inducted into the Hall of Fame, and at the time was a .321 career hitter. In 1906 he had led the league in triples, runs scored, and stolen bases. But he had been outhit by Cobb .320 to .306, and it was obvious that Cobb was also much faster, bigger, and stronger. The final clincher should have been that Flick, thirty-one, was considerably older than Cobb.

But Cleveland decided to turn down the offer, citing a concern for the harmony of their club. Ironically, Flick was also known for a hot temper. He had once gotten in a fight with Hall of Fame teammate Nap Lajoie and disabled the star second baseman for five weeks.

Cleveland's rejection of the trade was one of the worst baseball decisions of all time. In 1907 Ty Cobb began a string of nine straight batting titles and led the Tigers to three consecutive pennants, including 1908 when they edged out Cleveland by a single game.

And Elmer Flick? Well, in 1907 he hit a commendable .302, but that was still 48 points behind Cobb, who also had *twice* as many RBIs as Flick. Even worse for Cleveland, that was the last good year of Elmer's career. The next year Flick suffered a mysterious stomach ailment and hit only .254 in the remaining 338 at bats in his career.

From the day the Tigers made the offer, Elmer Flick hit .284 and Cobb hit .370. Flick had 252 hits and Cobb had *4,043!* Cleveland had turned down what would have been the greatest steal in baseball history.

After the Non-Trade										
	G	AB	H	B.A.	2B	3B	HR	SLUG%	R	RBI	SB
Flick	246	887	252	.284	28	22	4	.379	115	82	51
Cobb	2895	10929	4043	.370	705	209	116	.519	2181	1905	867

Tommy McCarthy,
the Thinking Man's Ballplayer

ommy McCarthy's playing record is hardly Hall of Fame material. He had a relatively short career before his retirement at age thirty-two. He played only eight major-league seasons in which he had as many as 400 at bats, and he was not a dominating hitter. He played in a heavy-hitting era from 1884 to 1896, but his career average is only .292, and he wasn't a power hitter.

When McCarthy was inducted into the Hall of Fame in 1946, it was largely a recognition of his role in making baseball a more scientific and finely skilled game. And it is fair to say that his contributions as a thinking ballplayer also made him a winning ballplayer.

In his eight seasons as a full-time regular with the St. Louis Browns and Boston Nationals, his teams took three pennants, never had a losing record, and posted an overall winning percentage of .634. That translates to an average of 103 wins in a modern schedule of 162 games.

Rather than have the coaches give signs to the players, McCarthy developed a practice in which the batter and runner signaled their intentions back and forth. Using these signs with Hall of Fame teammate Hugh Duffy, McCarthy worked out a play that became the now-common hit-and-run.

Tommy McCarthy.

THOMAS F. M'CARTHY, Outfielder
One of Boston's Heavenly Twins

When McCarthy reached second base he would use his signs to relay the catcher's pitch selection to the batter at the plate. This, too, was a baseball first. Although McCarthy was primarily an outfielder, he played over 100 games in the infield. It was there he invented the ploy of letting an infield fly drop with men on first and second, less than two outs and then starting a double play. This of course, led to the introduction of the modern infield-fly rule.

McCarthy's most famous defensive strategy was uniquely suited to the Dead-Ball Era. McCarthy was very fast and blessed with a strong throwing arm. In his era the ball was so dead that outfielders could play much closer to the infield, and a strong-armed outfielder could throw accurately on the fly to all the bases.

McCarthy constantly practiced charging the ball, fielding it on a short hop, and coming up throwing the ball to the appropriate base. The result was that a runner on first base could not run aggressively on any line drive near McCarthy. If the runner went more than halfway to second base, McCarthy might snare the line drive and get a double play on a strong throw to first. But if the runner played it safe by staying close to first base, McCarthy would short-hop the apparent hit and fire it into second base for the force out.

The risky play caused McCarthy to make an extra error or two, but in his eight seasons as a full-time player, he averaged 33 assists and eight double plays for every 150 games in the outfield. And that doesn't take into account the hundreds of runners he froze in their tracks, keeping them from taking an extra base. Underneath the playing record of Tommy McCarthy was a thinking ballplayer and a Hall of Fame innovator.

The Best
Turnaround Team
In Major-League History

The 1889 Louisville Colonels were an absolutely horrible team. They finished dead last with 27 wins and 111 losses for a winning percentage below .200. In 1890, the forming of the Players League caused some changes in the balance of the league, but close examination shows that the new league was only a minor factor in the miracle of Louisvile in 1890.

By a twist of fate, the players returning from the 1889 Colonels each had the absolute best years of their respective careers in 1890. Chicken Wolf, their right fielder, took the batting championship with an astounding .363 average. It was an amazing performance for Wolf, who had never hit over .300 in his eight previous major-league seasons.

Shortstop Phil Tomney entered the season with a career batting average of .198, yet he hit a career-high .277 in 1890. He also had a big year in the field as he led all shortstops in chances fielded cleanly per game.

The incredible magic of 1890 was just as strong on the pitching mound. Pitcher Red Ehret went from being a twenty-nine-game loser to a twenty-five-game winner as he dropped his ERA from 4.80 to 2.53. Scotty Stratton, who won only three games for the 1889 team, won thirty-four games in 1890 and took the only ERA title of his career.

The Colonels were last in batting average and ERA in 1889, but ranked first in both categories just a year later. The team went from last to first place with an all-time record improvement of sixty-one wins!

How did the Louisville Colonels fare in 1891? They fell as quickly as they had risen. Chicken Wolf, their surprise batting champion, saw his average fall over a hundred points from .363 to .253. Phil Tomney, the light-hitting shortstop who found his stroke in 1890, totally lost it in 1891 and was released. He never played in the majors again.

Scotty Stratton, who had just won thirty-four games and led the league in ERA, ended up with six wins and saw his ERA jump over a run and a half.

The club won only fifty-five games, a drop of thirty-three wins from their 1890 season, a total that left them in seventh place in the eight-team league. No other club in baseball history can match the roller coaster ride of the Louisville Colonels of 1889 through 1891.

	1889	1890	1891
Louisville Colonels	27-111	88-44*	55-84
Finish	EIGHTH	FIRST	SEVENTH
TEAM RUNS	632	819*	713
TEAM ERA	4.81	2.58*	4.27
CHICKEN WOLF'S B.A.	.291	.363*	.253
EHRET'S WINS & ERA	10, 4.80	25, 2.53	13, 3.47
STRATTON'S WINS & ERA	3, 3.23	34, 2.36*	6, 4.08

(*Led League)

Baseball's Strongest Hitter

abe Ruth hit home runs more frequently than any other major leaguer, but according to the players of his era, Jimmie Foxx hit the ball harder, farther, and faster than anyone else. Yes, faster. His manager Connie Mack noted that the muscular right-handed slugger hit a lot of line-drive homers and could get the ball out of the park faster than anyone. Lefty Gomez joked that you could get whiplash trying to follow a Foxx home run out of the park.

Yankee catcher Bill Dickey once said, "If I were catching blindfolded, I'd always know when it was Jimmie Foxx that connected. He hit the ball harder than anyone."

One American League rookie remembered that in every park he entered, people

Jimmie Foxx in 1944 with the Chicago Cubs.

would say that the longest home run hit there had come off the bat of Jimmie Foxx. Finally the rookie got a chance to personally see Foxx really connect with one, and he still couldn't believe what he saw. He exclaimed, "I've seen it with my own eyes, and it's a damn lie!"

Lefty Gomez said that Foxx hit the longest home run he ever gave up—along with the second, third, fourth, and fifth longest. The one Gomez remembered best was the blast that landed well into the third deck of left field in Yankee Stadium, which still had enough force to break the back of a wooden seat. Given the unusual depth of left field in Yankee Stadium, Foxx's home run was probably hit harder than the legendary Mantle home run that bounced off the rooftop facade in right field.

In Chicago they talk about the ball Foxx hit over the roof of Comiskey Park. The ball landed in a playground an estimated 600 or more feet from home plate.

Foxx won the fifth game of the 1930 World Series by breaking a scoreless tie with a ninth-inning blast that went all the way out of St. Louis' Sportsman's Park. It is believed to be the longest home run in World Series history.

In 1932 Foxx got a chance to set the all-time single-season home run record, but came up short due to some changes in ballpark architecture. After Babe Ruth hit his sixty homers in 1927, several ballparks began to make changes to stop some of the cheaper home runs.

In St. Louis, they erected a screen on top of their short right-field fence. Foxx—who always hit well in Sportsman's Park—hit that screen *five* times in 1932. Over in Cleveland's League Park, they erected a similar screen on their left-field wall, and they claim Foxx hit that screen at least three times the same year.

In 1932 Jimmie Foxx hit fifty-eight home runs, and it doesn't take a mathematical genius to figure that without these changes, Foxx easily would have surpassed Ruth's record with sixty-six homers or more. Although he missed the record, Foxx's fifty-eight homers remain the major-league record for a right-handed batter.

Jimmie Foxx's Assault on the Career Home Run Record

While most fans know that Jimmie Foxx made a serious run at the single-season all-time home run record with fifty-eight homers in 1932, few realize how long he kept up a pace that would have surpassed the career record of both Ruth and Aaron.

Like Ruth, Foxx got off to a late start as a home run hitter because he started off at the wrong position. While Ruth was hampered by beginning as a pitcher, Foxx was handicapped by starting out as a catcher. The real problem was that Foxx came to the big leagues with another catcher named Mickey Cochrane. Not only was Cochrane four years older with more minor-league experience, but he was one of the greatest catchers of all time.

During Foxx's first four years in the majors he was simply a highly talented utility player despite an impressive pinch-hitting average of .333 in forty-five tries and an overall batting average of .331. When he became the Athletics' regular first baseman in 1929, he began a record streak of twelve consecutive seasons with 30 homers or more, and he actually averaged better than 40 homers a year during that twelve-year run.

On September 24, 1940, Foxx hit his 500th career home run. He was still a month shy of his thirty-third birthday, and he remains the youngest player to ever reach that milestone. According to research by Bill James, he also had more career runs scored and more RBIs than any other player at the same age. Through age thirty-two he was 84 homers ahead of Ruth's pace and 58 homers ahead of Aaron's.

After age thirty-two, both Ruth and Aaron hit about 300 more homers. Jimmie Foxx? Well, in 1941 his awesome streak ended as he belted only 19 homers. The next year he hit only eight, and he had a batting average of .226, which was better than 100 points below his career average. Foxx suddenly retired at age thirty-four, although he came back briefly a couple of years later and added 8 more homers to his record. After age thirty-two, Foxx hit a total of only 34 homers.

Foxx's drastic drop in power after age thirty-two has never been tied to any visible injury. There are strong similarities between the decline of Foxx and that of another slugger, Hack Wilson. In Hack's case it is generally accepted that he drank away his reflexes with hard liquor.

Several of Foxx's contemporaries suggest this may also have happened to Jimmie, who preferred scotch to beer. During his career, Foxx claimed he could drink fifteen shots of scotch without being affected. This abuse may finally have caught up to his reflexes at age thirty-three. As it was, Foxx had a remarkable career, but he fell 221 homers and 376 RBIs short of the all-time records that, at age thirty-two, he seemed destined to own.

Addie Joss, Shooting Star

On April 26, 1902, baseball fans quickly learned that a new pitching star had entered the American League. Twenty-two-year-old Addie Joss turned in the most impressive debut of any rookie pitcher in baseball history. Pitching for Cleveland, he just missed a no-hitter and settled for a one-hit shutout over St. Louis.

In 1904, at age twenty-four, Joss had a 1.59 ERA, the lowest in either league. In 1907 he led the American League in wins with 27, and in 1908 he again led both leagues in ERA, this time with a 1.16 mark, the third-lowest ERA in league history.

In four consecutive seasons, from 1906 to 1909, Addie Joss' ERA was never higher than 1.83. He got off to a fine start in 1910 by throwing a no-hitter in his second start

Addie Joss

of the season, but he began to complain of soreness and fatigue. Joss ended up making only twelve starts and winning five games that season.

When Joss reported for spring training in 1911, he was seriously underweight and seemed to have no energy. During an exhibition game he fainted on the bench, and a few weeks later—just days after his thirty-first birthday—he died of tubercular meningitis.

Joss left behind an impressive record that included a career ERA of 1.88, which is the second-lowest in baseball history. Joss—who had exceptional control—is also baseball's all-time career leader in fewest base-runners allowed per inning. Yet sixty-five years after Joss had thrown his last pitch, he was still barred from the Hall of Fame. You see, Joss got in only nine major-league seasons before his sudden death, and the Hall of Fame has a ten-season requirement. A special exception to that rule was made in 1978 to place Addie Joss with his fellow baseball immortals.

Even without Hall of Fame election, Addie Joss would never have been forgotten, thanks to the game he pitched on October 2, 1908. In the closing weeks of that season, there was a fierce three-way pennant race between Detroit, Cleveland, and Chicago. On October 2, Addie Joss' Indians were trailing Detroit by just five percentage points. But Addie was pitching that day against Chicago's Big Ed Walsh, who had already won 40 games that season.

Walsh was brilliant, striking out fifteen and allowing only one run, which scored on an error and a wild pitch. But Joss was better—27 men up, 27 men down—with a perfect game, to win 1-0. Although the Tigers still managed to squeak by to win the pennant, Joss' perfect game under immense pressure became the pitching feat of the century.

In an odd twist of fate, when Addie's son Norman was in high school, his math teacher asked if he were related to Addie Joss, the perfect game pitcher. It turned out that Norman Joss' math teacher was John Richmond, the man who in 1880 had thrown the first perfect game in major-league history.

Professional Baseball's Youngest Player

For nearly twenty years the record for the youngest professional player belonged to Joe Schultz, who later became a major-league player, coach, and manager. Back in 1932 his father, Joe Schultz, Sr., managed the minor-league club in Houston and used his fourteen-year-old son as a pinch-hitter in the final game of the season.

On July 19, 1952, Joe Relford bumped Schultz from the record book when he appeared in an official minor-league game as a twelve-year-old. Relford was the batboy for Fitzgerald in the Georgia State League. With the team getting clobbered 13-0, the crowd began chanting, "Put in the batboy." Manager Charlie Ridgeway consulted with umpire Ed Kubick and received permission to send young Relford to the plate as a pinch-hitter. Little Joe managed to hit a sharp grounder to third base but was thrown out at first.

Fitzgerald left Relford in the game, playing him in center field. He did not get to bat again, but he did make what was described as "…a sensational catch of a line drive against the fence."

Unfortunately, Relford's appearance caused a considerable ruckus when the game report was received by the league office. When fourteen-year-old Joe Schultz went to the plate in 1932, it was considered the cute kind of stunt occasionally found in minor-league games. But when twelve-year-old Joe Relford got into a Georgia State League game, it was considered a catastrophe.

League president Bill Estrof fired umpire Ed Kubick for allowing Relford into the game. Fitzgerald manager Charlie Ridgeway was fined $50 and suspended for five days, and Joe Relford was dismissed from his batboy job a few days later.

The problem may not have been Relford's age but the fact that he was black. The use of a twelve-year-old boy in a professional contest was officially condemned for making a travesty of the game, but it is also true that Relford was the first to break the color line in the Class D Georgia State League.

Joe Relford was more than just baseball's youngest professional player. The players nicknamed him "Joe Louis" after the great black fighter, but in fact he was the Jackie Robinson of baseball in Georgia.

King Kelly
Rewrites the Rule Book

ne of the most colorful and intelligent ballplayers in the nineteenth century was Mike "King" Kelly. He was a superbly confident athlete who believed he could play any position, and did. Although primarily an outfielder and catcher, during his major-league career he played at least nine games at every position, including twelve appearances on the pitching mound.

Kelly's best years were with the Chicago Nationals, also known as the Chicago Colts and later as the Cubs. Kelly took the National League batting championship in both 1884 and 1886 and led the league in runs scored for three straight seasons.

Kelly was also tremendously popular with the fans and was immortalized in a popular song of the era titled "Slide, Kelly, Slide." After winning the 1886 batting title, King Kelly was sold to Boston for the incredible sum of $10,000, which was about half the value of a major-league franchise in those days. In his first five games with Boston he had more hits and scored more runs than the rest of the Boston team combined.

Yet the Kelly trade ended up haunting Boston. Even though Kelly was only twenty-nine years old at the time, his reflexes were already beginning to slow down due to a career of heavy drinking. By age thirty-two he was a part-time player, and thereafter hit only .244 in his career.

But when the old-timers remember Kelly, they don't talk about his great skills in his younger days or his sad decline, they remember his quick thinking on the playing field.

Mike "King" Kelly

One of Kelly's legendary "mind" plays came when he was catching with a runner on second and two outs. The runner had taken off with the pitch, which was hit for a routine grounder to the shortstop. The runner was rounding third and did not see that the shortstop had bobbled the ball, but he could see King Kelly tossing his catcher's glove to the dugout as if the third out had been made. When the runner slowed and started to turn toward the dugout, his teammates screamed at him that he had been tricked. Kelly called for the ball, which he caught barehanded, and tagged the confused runner.

When Kelly was player-manager of Boston, his quickness of mind actually led to a basic rule change. One day Kelly was on the bench when a foul pop-up was hit his way and beyond the reach of his catcher. Kelly jumped to his feet and yelled, "Kelly, now catching for Boston!", then caught the ball for a legal put-out. By the end of the season there was a new rule in the books limiting player substitutions to times when the ball is officially dead.

The Day the Dodgers
Put Three Men on Third Base

Imagine three men on third base. This is not an easy play to pull off. It should not be attempted at home, and it should be kept off the Little League diamonds whenever possible. Basically it takes a minimum of three base-running blunders and a total breakdown in communication from the third-base coach. But yes, it actually happened among the game's finest practitioners, the major leaguers.

It was August 15, 1926, in a game between the Brooklyn Dodgers and the Boston Braves. The score was tied at 1-1 in the seventh, but the Dodgers had loaded the bases with nobody out and had their best hitter, Babe Herman, at the plate. Babe lashed a hard shot into right field that looked good for a double, possibly a triple.

The runner on third base scored easily to give the Dodgers the lead, but that was quickly forgotten in the excitement at third base. The trouble started when pitcher Dazzy Vance, the runner on second, held up to make sure the ball wasn't going to be caught. Dazzy was never a fast runner and had thoughts of stopping at third even when he saw the ball fall in the gap.

With Vance tiptoeing into third base, coach Mickey O'Neil saw Chick Fewster, the runner from first base, barreling around second and heading for third. O'Neill waved frantically for Fewster to hold at second, but all he succeeded in doing was making sure Vance stopped at third. As Vance and Fewster looked at each other in confusion at third base, in slid Babe Herman, who thought he had cleared the bases and was going for a triple.

Fewster looked at the other two runners in disgust and walked to the dugout. Braves third baseman Andy High tagged all three runners and looked toward the umpire for the ruling on this once-in-a-lifetime play.

As all three runners were being tagged, Babe Herman was screaming at Dazzy Vance for his lousy base running. Vance replied that he might not be a smart runner, but he was smart enough to know he was the only one who was safe. And, indeed, he was the only runner entitled to the base. While many fans remember the play as the time Herman tripled into a triple play, he officially doubled into a double play.

The play was immortalized in a standard joke among Brooklyn fans. Whenever the Dodgers were reported to have three men on, someone was sure to inquire, "Oh yeah, which base?"

Eddie Rommel Goes
Out with a Game to Remember

E ddie Rommel had a fascinating career which spanned thirteen seasons (1920-32), all spent with the Philadelphia Athletics. He was one of the first knuckleballers to find success at an early age, and was using the pitch in the majors at age twenty-three in 1920.

The next year he was the Athletics' best pitcher, but he still led the league with 23 losses as the A's lost 100 games. The next year he completely turned it around and led the league in *wins* with 27. That remains the record for most wins by a pitcher in the twentieth century working for a team with a losing record.

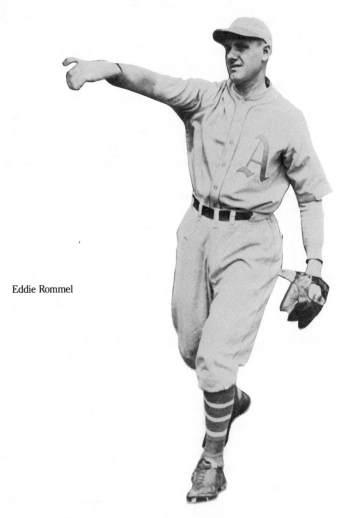

Eddie Rommel

The next year he again led the league in losses—nineteen—despite a slightly lower ERA than the year before. He is the only pitcher in baseball history to go through such a wild swing in three consecutive seasons.

As the Athletics slowly rebuilt into a powerhouse team, Rommel's record naturally began to improve. In 1925, he again led the league in wins, this time with 21, against only 10 losses. In the last five years of his career he became one of the game's first regular relievers. From 1928 to 1932, he pitched in relief in over 75 percent of his appearances. Twice he led the league in relief wins and had an impressive 23-8 record (.742) as a reliever.

The last win of his career came in relief, and surely it was one of the most unusual in the history of baseball. On July 10, 1932, the Athletics had to make a one-day road trip to Cleveland. The club had just played three straight doubleheaders and Connie Mack wanted to rest his pitching staff. He took only two pitchers on the trip: Lou Krause, who was to start the game, and reliever Eddie Rommel who would be a one-man bullpen.

Krause started the game but simply didn't have it, giving up three runs in the first inning. Even though Rommel had pitched three innings just the day before, Mack brought him in for the second inning. The game turned into a wild slugfest that somehow managed to go eighteen innings before Philadelphia won 18-17. Cleveland shortstop Johnny Burnett set an all-time record by collecting nine hits, but the real hero of the game was Ed Rommel, who had no choice but to pitch those final seventeen innings.

Rommel pitched to 87 batters, nearly ten times through the lineup, as he surrendered 14 runs and allowed a major-league record of 29 hits! But he did win the game, for what proved to be the final victory of his playing career. He retired at the end of the season and went on to a long and distinguished career as a major-league umpire who could truly say he had seen it all.

A Pair of
Intertwined Destinies

J oe Wilhoit, George Quellish, and Elam Vangilder are more than just a combined example of why proper names are not allowed in Scrabble. Their real story begins in 1919 with outfielder Joe Wilhoit's release by the New York Giants and move to the Wichita Witches of the Western League. Wilhoit got off to a fairly normal start, but then in mid-season it seemed that no one could get him out. He collected a hit in 69 consecutive games, during which he had an unbelievable batting average of .511! The longest hitting streak in professional baseball history came to an end on August 20, 1919. On the mound was twenty-three-year-old Elam Vangilder, who blanked Joe on a fly ball out, a ground out, and a swinging strike three.

Almost exactly ten years later, in another part of the country, minor leaguer George Quellish of the Reading Keys put together another all-time hitting streak, this one for most consecutive hits. Quellish had banged out thirteen consecutive hits going into the game of August 12, 1929. George singled in his first at bat and belted a grand slam in his second trip. Finally, in his third at bat he hit an easy fly out to end his record streak at fifteen consecutive hits.

And who was the pitcher on the mound? Would you believe it was Elam Vangilder, the same hurler who had ended Wilhoit's batting streak ten years earlier? The funny thing about Vangilder's becoming the great minor-league streak-buster is that Elam didn't spend a lot of time in the minors.

Vangilder had spent nearly all of the intervening ten years in the major leagues. After stopping Wilhoit's streak at 69 games in August of 1919, less than a month later Vangilder was in the major leagues pitching for the St. Louis Browns.

Elam started the next ten seasons in the majors where he was known as one of the best-hitting pitchers and a steady starter-reliever. In 1922, Vangilder won 19 games and hit .344, the eighth-highest batting average by a pitcher in American League history. In 1925 he led the league in relief wins with 11.

But in 1929 Vangilder got off to a rough start and was released by the Detroit Tigers. And so it happened that in August he found himself back in the minors facing George Quellish and his consecutive hits. Fate again had arranged for Vangilder to defend the honor of pitchers everywhere.

Baseball's 450-strikeout Season

The major-league record in this century for strikeouts in a season belongs to Nolan Ryan who whiffed 383 batters for the California Angels in 1973. He did it in 326 innings for an average of 10.6 strikeouts per nine innings.

As amazing as that record sounds, it is a far cry from the all-time major-league record. That belongs to Matches Kilroy with 513 way back in 1886. Of course, he also pitched 589 innings. In this century Rube Vickers struck out 409 batters in 1906, but he too pitched over 500 innings.

As baseball pitchers began throwing fewer and fewer innings, it seemed that no pitcher at any level would throw enough innings to collect 400 strikeouts in a single season. Then in 1938, a nineteen-year-old right-hander made his professional debut by whiffing 418 batters in the Alabama-Florida League.

That incredible performance was turned in by Virgil Trucks, who went on to pitch eighteen years in the majors. Because Trucks had to average 13.8 strikeouts per nine innings to snare that record, there was speculation that it would be the last of the 400-strikeout seasons. But just eight years later, in 1946, along came a husky, 200-pound left-hander named Bill Kennedy.

Pitching for Rocky Mount, Tennessee, in the Coastal Plains League, Kennedy obliterated Trucks' record by striking out 456 batters! That remains the professional record for this century, and Kennedy is the last American to break the 400 barrier in

Bill Kennedy at 21, a two-sport star at Temple University.

this century. (Yutaka Enatsu of Japan became the fourth pitcher in this century to strike out 400 batters in a professional baseball league when he whiffed 401 in 1968.)

What makes Kennedy's record so impressive is that it was done in only 280 innings, an average of 14.7 strikeouts for every nine innings. Kennedy ended up winning 28 games with only 3 losses and led the league with a 1.03 ERA.

Although Bill Kennedy rewrote the record book with his amazing 456 strikeouts in 1946, he never enjoyed the kind of major-league success that Virgil Trucks found. At age twenty-six, Kennedy began to experience some arm trouble. His exceptional velocity became inconsistent and he had trouble getting his pitches over the plate. In 1948, Cleveland brought him to the majors, but he was the wildest pitcher in the league, averaging well over 7 walks per nine innings.

He continued to pitch poorly but there was always another team willing to take a chance on the pitcher who had struck out 456 batters in a single season. He was traded five times and played in eight major-league seasons with Cleveland, St. Louis, Washington, Chicago, Boston, and Cincinnati. When he was finally released at age thirty-seven, his major-league career consisted of just 15 victories and 28 defeats, and a career ERA of 4.71. In 465 innings he struck out only 256 batters, exactly 200 less than in his record-setting minor-league season.

Bruno Haas
and the 1915 Athletics

I n 1914, Connie Mack's Philadelphia Athletics won 99 games to capture the American League pennant. But despite the team's success, the club was barely breaking even financially. With competition from the Federal League causing higher salaries, and with several of his stars threatening to jump to the new league, Connie Mack decided to sell off his top players and give Philadelphia a taste of budget baseball.

The team lost five Hall of Famers—Eddie Collins, Home Run Baker, Chief Bender, Eddie Plank, and Herb Pennock—and then lost 109 games in 1915 to finish 58½ games out of first place. That is the worst fall by a first-place club in major-league history.

The Athletics' offense dropped off over 200 runs, but that was nothing compared to the shelling their new pitching staff took. Mack worked desperately to put together some sort of pitching staff but nothing seemed to work. Only one pitcher worked over 200 innings and no less than twenty-seven different pitchers took the mound for the 1915 A's.

Philadelphia's pitching staff allowed nearly 200 runs more than the next worst staff in the league; they allowed *370* more runs than their 1914 team. 1915 was a good pitcher's year; the whole league had an ERA of 2.94, and no team had an ERA above 3.13—except for Philadelphia. The Athletics turned in an ERA of 4.33 which was *2.20 runs higher* than any other team in the league.

If any one event symbolized the desperation of Connie Mack and the A's, it was the major-league debut of pitcher Bruno Haas. On June 23, 1915, Mack gave the ball to Haas, a young college pitcher. His start against the New York Highlanders (later named the Yankees) was not only his first appearance in the majors but also his first appearance as a professional at any level of play.

The chunky southpaw added new meaning to the word "wild." Haas gave up 15 runs on 11 hits, three wild pitches, and a major-league record of *sixteen* walks.

It wasn't just nerves that led to Haas' wildness. In 1915 he pitched five more times in relief and in just 5⅓ innings he walked *twelve* more! He never appeared in the majors again and left behind a career ERA of 11.93 and an average of 17.6 walks for every nine innings pitched.

Bruno even swore off pitching when he arrived in the minor leagues. When Haas reported to the New York State League in 1916, he immediately switched to the outfield. Later, in 1921, he took up professional football and became one of the rare athletes who played in both the major leagues and the National Football League.

It was a wise career choice when Bruno Haas decided to "walk" away from pitching.

Smead Jolley,
the Original
All-Hit, No-Field Ballplayer

Smead "Smudge" Jolley was an awesome hitter in the 1930s, but there was no place for him in the field. The former pitcher had a strong arm, but he was a slow, clumsy fielder with an iron glove. Playing in the Pacific Coast League, he had a four-year average of .385 with 35 homers and 160 RBIs, but it wasn't until 1930, when he was twenty-eight years old, that Jolley got his chance to play in the majors.

Smead immediately became the starting right fielder for the Chicago White Sox, where he hit .313 and led the team with 114 RBIs. But his defense was so bad that he became a part-time player the next season even though he hit over .300 again and led the league in pinch-hits, with a .476 pinch-hitting average.

Smead Jolley

The next year Jolley was traded to the Red Sox, where he hit .312 and drove in 106 runs. But they too were unhappy with his defense and made him a platoon player the following season. He had an off year with a .282 average and was released.

Jolley was only thirty-two years old; he had a career average of .305; his pinch-hitting average was .385, and he had driven in over 100 runs in both of his full major-league seasons. But Smead never played another game in the majors. He returned to the minors where he played another eight years with a batting average of .353, including four batting titles, winning the last one when he was thirty-nine.

Old "Smudge" had to have some kind of ugly glove for a bat like that to be returned to the minors. Both Chicago and Boston have a favorite story of Jolley's fielding ineptness. Once, when he was with the White Sox, a single to left field bounced between Jolley's legs. When he turned to play it off the wall, the ball caromed back between his legs. He finally tracked it down—and then heaved it over the third baseman's head.

When Jolley first joined the Red Sox, the coaches hit a lot of deep fly balls to him so he could practice going up the ten-foot incline that served as a sort of warning track to the left-field wall. On the first deep fly in a game, Jolley dashed up the hill and discovered that he had misjudged the ball, which was going to fall thirty feet in front of him. He started to run back down the hill and fell flat on his face. Nonplussed, Jolley told the coaches, "For ten days you taught me how to go uphill, but none of you had the brains to teach me how to come down."

Smead Jolley—born to D.H., but born forty years too soon.

Baseball's Worst Defensive Outfielder?

Al "Kip" Selbach was an interesting figure in major-league baseball around the turn of the century. He had a highly unusual build, packing 190 pounds on his five-foot-seven-inch frame, but Kip was surprisingly fleet-footed. In 1895 he led the National League with 22 triples, and during his career he averaged thirty-one steals for every 150 games. Overall, he was a capable hitter with seven .300 seasons and a career average of .293.

But Kip Selbach never led the league in anything, and his only red-letter contributions to the record book are two disastrous days in the field. On August 19, 1902, he dropped three flyballs in left field and erred twice while picking up singles to tie the major-league record of five errors by an outfielder in a single game.

Two years later, on June 23, 1904, he made the book again as he dropped a fly, misplayed a single, and made a wild throw. This time he did it all in one inning to tie another major-league record.

But was Kip Selbach really that bad a fielder?

Those records only prove that Kip had his bad days in the field. His overall record is far from that of a bad outfielder or even an error-prone one. He was a good enough glove-man that his teams occasionally had him fill in at shortstop, where he played twenty-six games during his career. As a left fielder, he had very good range, and in 1898 he actually led the league in chances fielded cleanly per game.

Selbach's error totals and fielding averages were pretty normal. In his thirteen seasons, he never led the league in fielding percentage, but he never led in errors, either. In fact, the year he made the three errors in one inning, his fielding average of .961 was second best among the league's left fielders.

No major leaguer has ever had a worse day or a worse inning in the outfield than Kip Selbach, but under closer examination it's clear he was a much better fielder than his reputation suggests.

Heinie Zimmerman and Baseball's Most Expensive Temper

H enry "Heinie" Zimmerman was an extremely talented ballplayer, who some claim trailed only Home Run Baker as the best third baseman of the Dead-Ball Era.

In a thirteen-year career, Zimmerman played on three pennant winners, took one batting title, and led the league in RBIs three times. Playing with the Chicago Cubs in 1912, he became the first National League player in this century to win the Triple Crown.

Heinie was notorious for being combative and foul-tempered. As a twenty-one-year-old utility infielder with the 1908 Cubs, he set off one of the fiercest clubhouse fights of all time. At one point in the fight, Zimmerman hurled a bottle that caught star left fielder Jimmy Sheckard right between the eyes and nearly cost him his eyesight. Zimmerman then slugged it out with manager Frank Chance before being gang tackled by the rest of the club.

After Zimmerman's Triple Crown year in 1912, Heinie relied on his star status to vent his foul temper without penalty. The problem was that the umpires could care less that he was a star. On June 15, umpire Bill Klem ejected Zimmerman for arguing ball and strike calls. That wouldn't have been so unusual except that Heinie wasn't even the batter at the plate. When Klem gave Zimmerman the heave-ho from the bench, it was Heinie's fifth ejection of the year and his third in five days, which is still a record.

That ejection inspired one wealthy fan to try to control Zimmerman's temper by appealing to his other vice, greed. The fan sent half of a one-hundred-dollar bill to Zimmerman and the other half to a trusted sportswriter. Zimmerman was to get the second half of the C-note only if he could avoid being ejected for two weeks.

Heinie made a real effort to lay off the umpires and won the $100, but it turned out to be a losing proposition. When he could no longer vent his frustrations on the umpires he turned on his teammates, and when he made the mistake of yelling at manager Johnny Evers, he was slapped with a $250 fine.

Unfortunately, that wasn't the last time Zimmerman's temper cost him dearly. Heinie was traded to the Giants in 1916 and by 1919 had become a very bitter

Heinie Zimmerman

---

ballplayer. He was thirty-two years old and looking at the downside of his baseball career. His talents were beginning to slip away, and he was feuding with the New York Giants over his contract. He was convinced that the Giants were taking advantage of him, complaining that they were too quick to cut his contract after an off year in 1918. Heinie would work himself into a towering rage by pointing out that just two years before he had led the Giants to the pennant by leading the league in RBIs.

Zimmerman let his anger and thirst for money get the best of him. He became an easy target for the black-hearted Hal Chase, who probably fixed more games than any player in that shady era of baseball. In 1919, Chase joined the Giants and was looking for a partner to help him bribe several key Giants to throw baseball games. Zimmerman was his man.

Heinie and Hal were turned in by their teammates and banned from baseball for life. It was a sudden but not so surprising end to the tempestuous career of Heinie Zimmerman.

The Most Lopsided
Game In Baseball History

t was played on June 15, 1902 in the Texas League, and it has become the most famous game in minor-league history. The Corsicana Oilers, the first-place powerhouse team, was scheduled to host last-place Texarkana, but due to local laws forbidding baseball on Sunday, the contest had to be shifted to a small park in neighboring Ennis, Texas.

In their temporary quarters, the Oilers belted out 53 hits, including 16 homers, to totally crush Texarkana. Player-manager Big Mike O'Conner collected 7 hits including 3 homers and a triple, but the real star of the game was the Oilers' nineteen-year-old rookie catcher Nig Clarke.

The Ennis ballpark had a very short right-field fence, only about 210 feet from home plate. Clarke was a switch-hitter, and with a right-hander on the mound he drove *eight* straight balls over the short fence for 8 homers and *twenty* RBIs!

The Oilers were obviously enjoying running up the score. Despite a lead of 17-1 after three innings, they stole five bases and, as was the custom of the day, took their last at bats even though they were the home team. They scored eight more times in that last inning to win 51-3! When the final score went out over the wire, some telegraph operators refused to believe the 51-3 score and reported it as a 5-3 victory.

Over the years, too much has been made of the fact that the ballpark in Ennis was undersized and unusually short in right field. Lucky Wright, Corsicana's pitcher, did not give up a single home run and held Texarkana to nine hits and just three runs.

The key factor in this crazy game was Texarkana's pitcher. The story goes that the losing pitcher for Texarkana was not a regular member of the team. He was the son of C. B. DeWitt, who was part-owner of the club. Junior DeWitt reported to the manager and declared, "Papa said for me to pitch."

And pitch he did. He threw the whole nine innings and faced over 80 batters, which means he probably threw somewhere between 200 and 300 pitches. He did manage to strike out one Corsicana player who was lucky his teammates even let him back into the dugout.

Junior DeWitt did not get much fielding support from his Texarkana teammates. Although he allowed nearly 60 men to reach base, they turned only one double play. They also committed five errors, and one boxscore claims *25* of the runs were unearned.

Let's face it: the whole Texarkana team was bad, and it's no surprise that the club folded at the end of the 1902 season. On the site of their old ballpark sits the Texarkana Casket Company—a fitting reminder of the time Corsicana buried Texarkana, 51-3.

Going Beyond the Call of Duty

arry "Rube" Vickers stood six-feet-two and weighed 225 pounds, which made him look like a giant back at the turn of the century when the majority of hitters weighed around 160 pounds. But Vickers was a good-natured soul, always willing to do what he could to help his club.

In 1902, the Cincinnati Reds were in a jam when all their catchers became too banged up to play. They asked the big rookie pitcher to go behind the plate and catch a game. Rube was willing, but that one game was the full extent of his catching career as he allowed six passed balls in the game, a record that stood for 85 years.

In 1908, the Philadelphia Athletics talked him into pitching double duty as he made 33 starts and 20 relief appearances in the same season. In fact, he led the league with six wins in relief while also leading his team with 21 complete games.

Vickers was no stranger to such hard work. Two years earlier, in 1906, he had set an all-time record for innings pitched in a season. Pitching for Seattle in the Pacific Coast League, he had made *64* starts and become the only pitcher ever to throw

George "Zip" Zabel

over 500 innings in a season at the modern pitching distance of sixty feet, six inches which was established in 1893. Vickers won 39 games and struck out 409 batters while throwing an amazing 517 innings.

When Rube Vickers retired in 1915, reliever George "Zip" Zabel took up Rube's motto of "I'll do what it takes to get the job done." On June 17, 1915, Zabel's Chicago Cubs were playing the Brooklyn Dodgers. The Cubs' starting pitcher had to be pulled after retiring only two Dodger players.

Out of the bullpen came "Zip" Zabel. The twenty-four-year-old right-hander took the ball and went all the way to complete a 4-3 victory—in nineteen innings. That's right; the game went *ten* extra innings and Zip Zabel never left the game. In one relief appearance he pitched the equivalent of two complete games; his 18⅓ innings remains the longest relief appearance in baseball history.

Zip Zabel and Rube Vickers—remembered for going beyond the call of duty.

The Life
and Death of Rube Waddell

ne of the popular beliefs in baseball is that left-handed pitchers rarely have both oars in the water. Probably the zaniest lefty of them all was Hall of Famer Rube Waddell.

Connie Mack managed in the majors for 53 years and felt that, of all his pitchers, Waddell had the best combination of speed, curveball, and control. Rube pitched only ten full seasons in the majors, yet seven times he led his league in strikeouts. His 349 strikeouts in 1904 stood out not only as the highest total of the Dead-Ball Era, but as the strikeout record for over sixty years until broken by Sandy Koufax in 1965. Waddell twice led the league in ERA and retired with a career ERA of 2.16, the sixth-lowest mark in baseball history.

Waddell also had an amazing ability to live in a world of his own. He exasperated his managers frequently by showing up late at the ballpark, and sometimes not showing up at all. Sometimes he was off fishing or playing marbles with a bunch of kids. Frequently he was involved in his passion of chasing fire engines.

During his longer absences he was generally sampling new careers. He tried vaudeville and acted in a stage play. Once they found him tending bar, but the best laugh came when they found him working as a professional alligator wrestler.

There are several indicators that Waddell was probably mentally retarded, but he was fortunate enough to walk the world in a time when society looked more kindly upon a child in a man's body. He was handsome, and in his day he could still be a hero, an adverturesome character, and, yes, a Hall of Fame performer.

There was never any malice in Rube's actions. He had a natural inclination to help others, and it was this side of his nature which led to his premature death. Early in 1912, Waddell was visiting a friend in Hickman, Kentucky, when the town was threatened by the flooding Mississippi River. Waddell joined the town's efforts to lessen the damage by building a sandbag embankment, and spent several hours toiling in icy water up to his shoulders.

Rube caught a bad cold and never regained his health. He contracted tuberculosis and slowly wasted away. He died in the spring of 1914 at the age of thirty-seven.

Let the record show that the kindhearted Rube Waddell was more than just a free spirit.

Rube Waddell

Candy Cummings
Invents the Curveball

I n 1863, with the Civil War raging in the South, fourteen-year-old William Arthur Cummings was on a Brooklyn beach throwing clam shells into the surf. Fascinated with the way the shells would curve when thrown at the right angle with a snap of the wrist, young William became convinced he could somehow learn to make a baseball curve on its way to the plate.

It took four years of effort, but Cummings finally succeeded in learning how to make his pitches curve at will, with a reasonable measure of control. He was recruited by the famous Brooklyn Excelsiors as a marginal player, but his curveball —as the pitch was immediately dubbed—quickly made Cummings their best pitcher as well as leading attraction.

With the curveball such a basic pitch in modern baseball, it is difficult to imagine the stir that Cummings caused over 120 years ago. Large crowds turned out whenever he pitched, and even President Andrew Johnson went to see Cummings make the ball mysteriously curve in the air.

The new pitch gave Cummings a tremendous edge against hitters, and he quickly became the star hurler in the New York area. In those days "candy" was a slang term meaning "the best," and William Cummings quickly became known as "Candy" Cummings.

When the National Association, baseball's first professional league, completed its inaugural season in 1871, famed sportswriter Henry Chadwick called Candy Cummings the "outstanding pitcher" in the country. Oddly enough, at the time, Cummings' "freak" pitch was technically illegal. The rules required that the ball be pitched with a "stiff wrist." However, the umpires claimed they could not tell whether Cummings was or was not snapping his wrist. In 1872 the rule was changed and the curveball became a permanent part of baseball.

Cummings remained a star pitcher during the league's five-year existence. When the National League formed in 1876 he was still a solid pitcher, but his performance began to slip dramatically the very next season. In 1877, Cummings won only 5 games against 14 defeats. He was only 28 years old, but he never again pitched in the majors. Fourteen years of countless curveballs had taken their toll on the arm of the slightly built, 120-pound pitcher.

Cummings was extremely proud of his role in discovering and establishing the curveball. Even in retirement he would get up and demonstrate the pitch at the drop of a hat. In 1910, when he was over sixty years old, he pitched in an Old-Timers Game in Boston. To the delight of the crowd the tiny grey-haired gentleman snapped off several roundhouse curves.

With his induction into the Hall of Fame in 1939, there is no chance that baseball will ever forget Candy Cummings, the Father of the Curveball.

The Homer in the Gloaming

B ack in the days before night baseball, sportswriters had plenty of opportunity to use the poetic Scottish word "gloaming," which means twilight. Sunset was a significant factor in the drama of many a game. All the old-timers can remember pitching duels in which opposing pitchers would lock horns in extra innings and battle until the sky turned dark and left the game a tie. And the sports pages were full of baseball heroics which prevented games from being lost to darkness. None became more famous than the blow struck on September 28, 1938.

The Pittsburgh Pirates had started the month with a 6½ game lead over Chicago. The Cubs had whittled that lead down to half a game when the teams met for the second game of a head-to-head series in Wrigley Field. The Pirates took a 5-3 lead into the eighth. Timely hitting and a key pinch-hit by Tony Lazzeri tied the game at 5-5, but then Paul Warner, the Pirate right fielder, threw out the go-ahead run at the plate. By the bottom of the ninth the sun was beginning to sink below the horizon. It looked as if the Pirates would remain in first place and force a doubleheader the next day.

The first two Cubs went out easily, and only Gabby Hartnett, the Cubs' thirty-eight-year-old player-manager, was left to prevent the game from being called because of darkness. The hometown crowd groaned as Hartnett swung and missed, then fouled off the next pitch for a quick two strikes. Pirate pitcher Mace Brown came back with an 0-2 curveball, Gabby gave a mighty swing and the ball was gone into the falling twilight. It was so dark that Hartnett knew only from the feel of the blow that it was launched into the bleachers. Out of the dusky darkness came an answering roar, and everyone knew the Cubs were in first place.

Gabby Hartnett's twilight homer in 1938 gave the Cubs a lead they would not relinquish, and produced the fourth pennant in Hartnett's career with the Cubs. That dramatic homer became entrenched in baseball lore as "The Homer In the Gloaming." It still holds a special significance for Cub fans who consider it their last legitimate pennant. With the exception of the tainted 1945 war-year win, the Cubs have gone over fifty years without a pennant.

Many long-time Cub fans opposed the installation of lights at Wrigley Field because they kept hoping for another heroic twilight performance to save them from their pennantless fate. With light towers finally erected in 1988, there will be no more "Homers in the Gloaming."

The 1899 Cleveland Spiders, the Worst Team in Baseball History

P rior to 1899, the Cleveland Spiders of the National League had a string of seven straight winning seasons. In a highly unethical move, the Robison brothers, who owned the Cleveland club, bought a second National League team, the original St. Louis Browns. They decided that St. Louis would be a better baseball town and proceeded to trade the heart of their Cleveland club to St. Louis.

In fact, they traded Cleveland's entire pitching staff, which included a star hurler named Cy Young. They also transferred Cleveland's two best hitters, Hall of Famers Jesse Burkett and Bobby Wallace. That was great for the St. Louis team, which improved its record by a remarkable forty-five wins, but the team left in Cleveland was an absolute joke.

How bad were they? Well, the best pitcher they received from St. Louis was "Cold Water" Jim Hughey who did lead the team in wins and ERA. But big deal! "Cold Water" Jim won only four games and had a 5.41 ERA. He also managed to lead the league with thirty losses.

Former Spider pitcher Cy Young won 26 games for St. Louis. The *entire* Spiders team won only 20 games!

Yes, the 1899 Spiders finished with a record of 20 and 134. They were outscored by better than a two-to-one margin and finished a record 84 games out of first place.

Six times they had a losing streak of ten games or more. Manager Lave Cross quit in disgust when the club started off by going 8 and 30. Actually that was the club's

The 1898 Cleveland Spiders, the best of whom (including Cy Young, in the striped shirt) became St. Louis Browns the next season.

high-water mark as they lost over 100 more games with just 12 more wins. There was one game in which Cleveland jumped out to a surprising 10-1 lead over Brooklyn, but in true Spider fashion came back in the late innings to pull out the loss, 11-10.

The Cleveland fans were not willing to pay to see this kind of baseball, so the Robison brothers gave up the rights to thirty-six of their home games and had them played on the road. The Spiders were literally run out of town as they never played a game in Cleveland after August 30.

They thought it couldn't get any worse, but they were wrong. In their last forty-one games, the Spiders won only once, going 1-40. Their last game was in Cincinnati, where they recruited their hotel clerk to pitch against the Reds. They lost 19-3, and it was the last time the Spiders would be stepped on. The next year the Cleveland franchise was mercifully barred from the National League.

Baseball's
Left-handed Shortstop

Back in the 1800s, when teams generally carried only twelve to fifteen players, baseball saw a number of left-handed throwers pressed into emergency duty at shortstop. But only one major-league team has used a left-handed thrower as their *regular* shortstop.

In 1896, the Phillies' player-manager Billy Nash felt he had to replace his shortstop Boots Sullivan, who was coming off a season where he made sixty-two errors in just 95 games. Nash moved Sullivan to the outfield and decided to install rookie Billy Hulen at shortstop. And, yes, Hulen was a left-hander in both batting and throwing.

Nash's handling of the team was rather suspect right from the beginning. A left-handed shortstop was throwing often to a first baseman who would become one of the greatest second basemen of all time. Rookie Nap Lajoie appeared in thirty-nine games with the Phillies and played first base in every one.

The experiment with Hulen was far from a success. Hulen's range was limited and his fielding percentage was even slightly worse than Boots Sullivan's had been in 1895. Oddly enough, the lefty did turn out to be reasonably adept on double plays.

The Phillies' ace pitcher, Brewery Jack Taylor, set a milestone of sorts by winning twenty games with a left-handed thrower at shortstop, but the future was not rosy for the participants in this odd episode. A curse seemed to descend on the Phillies for violating tradition by using a left-handed shortstop.

The next year player-manager Billy Nash was told to shut up and just play third base; he never again managed in the majors. Boots Sullivan was traded in mid-season and died the next year at age twenty-seven—hopefully not from the embarrassment of being the only major leaguer to lose his job to a left-handed shortstop.

And Brewery Jack Taylor, the man who won twenty games with a left-handed shortstop, developed a kidney disorder and died four years later at age twenty-six. Is it any wonder no one uses a left-handed shortstop anymore? This history reads like the script of *The Curse of the Mummy*.

As for the player himself, Billy Hulen went on to play one more year as a backup shortstop with the National League club in Washington, D.C. He lived to the ripe old age of seventy-seven, and probably spent most of those years trying to convince people that Lefty Billy Hulen really did play shortstop in the major leagues.

The Miracle Braves of 1914

The Boston Braves of 1914 were dubbed the "Miracle Braves" because of the amazing pennant race which saw them lingering in last place as late as July 19. From that point, they gained an incredible 21½ games on the New York Giants.

But the Boston miracle was expected to end in the World Series where they would take on the powerhouse teams of the era, the Philadelphia Athletics. Connie Mack's A's were defending world champions and this was their fourth pennant in five years. Their roster included five future Hall of Famers, and many newspapermen were predicting the first four-game sweep in Series history.

Hank Gowdy

It was hard to take the Braves as serious challengers. Their outfield was so weak that manager George Stallings had to weave an elaborate platoon system where no single outfielder managed even 400 at bats. Butch Schmidt was the club's leading hitter at .295 while Philadelphia had three of the top six hitters in the American League. That trio of Eddie Collins, Stuffy McInnis, and Home Run Baker combined for a .325 average covering nearly 1700 at bats.

Well, the handicappers of the 1914 World Series were correct in predicting the first sweep in World Series history, but they backed the wrong team. The Miracle Braves stunned the cocky Athletics with strong pitching. The hard-hitting offense from Philadelphia had led all of baseball with a team batting average of .272, but in the fall classic they hit exactly 100 points less and scored only six runs against a no-name pitching staff of Dick Rudolph, Bill James, and Lefty Tyler.

The most valuable player of the Series was the young catcher who so masterfully guided the no-name pitching staff. Twenty-four-year-old Hank Gowdy had hit only .243 with three homers in the regular season, but he absolutely crushed the ball in the World Series. He hit a remarkable .545, including the Series' only homer and only triple. In fact, only one of his six hits in eleven at bats was a single. Despite playing with the dead ball of that era, his slugging percentage was well over a thousand (1.273). Naturally enough, he led both teams in runs scored and RBIs.

Ironically, when Gowdy got into a second World Series in 1923, he went hitless in three games. The next year he played in his third and final World Series, hitting only .259 with all singles. But in 1914 he was unstoppable, giving a miracle performance that crowned a miraculous year for the Boston Braves.

What's in a Name?

M any things go into the making of a ballplayer; often, talent is not enough. There was one player who nearly missed out on a big-league career because of the size of his ears.

Cliff Melton was a left-handed pitcher from the small town of Black Mountain, North Carolina. He was the best amateur pitcher in the area, and a bit of a local celebrity. Because he stood six-feet-six, the local newspapers gave him the impressive title of "The Towering Cliff of Black Mountain." Unfortunately, the big leaguers would not be so kind in assigning him a nickname.

Melton was signed to a minor-league contract by the New York Giants and in 1935 attended his first big-league training camp. One day, the nervous rookie was struggling to keep his composure while pitching in an exhibition game against the Cubs, who were notorious for "bench jockeying"—riding a player in hopes of breaking his spirit or concentration. Besides his height, Melton's most obvious physical feature was a pair of floppy, jug-handle ears. Gabby Hartnett of the Cubs yelled out, "Hey, Mickey Mouse, tie up those ears so I can see the outfield!" And that became the rookie's nickname.

Well, being known as Mickey Mouse Melton did not do a lot for the country boy's confidence, and he was quickly farmed out to the minors where the nickname continued to hound him. The nickname embarrassed the youngster, causing him to duck his head and pitch more passively. Finally, his minor-league manager told Melton that if he didn't like the nickname, he should do something about it.

Melton took him at his word. In his next start opposing manager Ray Schalk called him "Mickey Mouse," and the 205-pound Melton charged into the opposing dugout and punched Schalk's lights out. When the league fined Melton, his club not only paid the fine but gave Cliff a $100 bonus.

Before his next start, another player called Melton "Mickey Mouse" and again Melton knocked the offender cold. Before long the nickname lost its appeal and Melton was back on his way to the majors.

Melton's renewed aggressiveness buried the "Mickey Mouse" nickname for good, and Cliff joined the Giants in 1937. He pulled off the rare feat of not only winning twenty games in his rookie season but also leading the league with seven saves.

Melton also picked up a nickname he could live with. He liked to play the guitar in his spare time and had a weakness for singing country ballads. For the rest of his career the boy from Black Mountain, North Carolina, was known as "Mountain Music" Melton.

What's in a name? For pitcher Cliff Melton it was the difference between the minors and the majors.

Duke Bresnahan Turns the Catcher Into an Iron Man

hen Roger "Duke" Bresnahan was elected to the Hall of Fame, his position was listed as catcher, although Duke's transition to a full-time catcher took several years. He started off as an eighteen-year-old pitcher who threw a shutout in his very first major-league game and won all four of his pitching decisions in his rookie season. But young Roger also hit .375 and ended up pitching only three more games in his seventeen-year career.

Besides being a strong hitter, Bresnahan was a great fielder with a rocket arm and, despite his stocky build of 200 pounds on a five-foot-nine frame, he was remarkably fast. Through age twenty-five he actually played center field more often than any other position. It was Christy Mathewson who finally convinced Roger to become the New York Giants' regular catcher in 1905.

Bresnahan was an immediate success behind the plate, thanks to his agility, strong arm, and highly regarded baseball "smarts." In his first World Series, Bresnahan caught Mathewson's record setting *three* shutouts. The Athletics managed only two steals and scored only three runs in the five-game series. Duke was also a hitting star in the Series as he stroked the ball for a .313 average while the rest of the Giants averaged just .197.

But Bresnahan still had some doubts about whether he should continue catching. He wasn't thrilled with the aches and pains that routinely went with the position. In that era, the protective equipment was so primitive that even the most durable catchers were lucky to play 100 games in a season, and they frequently had their

Roger "Duke"
Bresnahan in 1909.

careers shortened by repeated injuries.

Although it was considered unmanly, several catchers began wearing felt pads under their stockings to protect their shins against foul tips. In 1907 Bresnahan brought the issue out of the closet by designing and wearing padded metal guards to protect his shins and knees while catching.

Bresnahan is generally recognized as the father of shinguards, but few know he also improved the standard catcher's mask by adding extra padding in strategic spots. With the endorsement of a star like Bresnahan, the new equipment quickly caught on and caused a dramatic improvement in the durability of catchers. In 1907 the starters in the major leagues averaged only 90 games behind the plate, and no catcher had more than 115 games. The all-time record belonged to Chief Zimmer who caught 125 games back in 1890.

Yet in 1908, no less than *six* catchers surpassed Zimmer's record, including 139 games behind the plate by Roger Bresnahan, the man who made the catcher an everyday player.

Brakeman Jack Taylor
Finished What He Started

J ack Taylor's nickname came from his work as a railroad brakeman in the off-season, but he easily could have earned the name from his ability to finish a game.

Brakeman Jack was a solid enough pitcher during his 10-year career. Four times he won 20 games, twice doing it with losing clubs. In 1902, he was the Cubs' best pitcher, responsible for 22 of their 68 wins as he led the league with a 1.33 ERA and eight shutouts. Yet Taylor earned his special place in baseball history with his durability rather than the quality of his pitching.

Brakeman Jack, a native of Straightville, Ohio, had a simple philosophy when it came to pitching: a man ought to finish what he starts. In Jack's first 100 games as a starting pitcher, he failed to throw a complete game only twice. In 1902 he started a streak that would cover five years and produce a string of *187* consecutive complete games. Now *there's* a record that will never be broken!

Think about what it would take to complete 187 straight games. What do you do when the game hits extra innings? If you're Jack Taylor, you finish the game. Early in the streak, on June 22, 1902, Taylor went into extra innings with a 2-2 tie. *Ten* innings later he walked off the field with a 3-2 victory in nineteen innings. Later on in the streak he had another complete game that went eighteen innings.

Further research has shown that Taylor also made fifteen relief appearances during the streak, finishing each game. That meant Taylor made over 200 consecutive pitching appearances without ever being relieved.

The streak finally came to an end late in 1906. Brakeman Jack pitched well for the Chicago Cubs through the first two-thirds of the season, but then in Brooklyn, on August 12, the Dodgers—who had the worst batting average in the league (.232)—stunned the crowd by knocking Taylor out of the game in the *third inning.* That ended Taylor's streak of 202 appearances without relief help. It was also a sign of tough times ahead.

Taylor's arm had begun to go lame. Thanks to his strong start he managed to win twenty games, but he did not pitch a single inning for the Cubs in the 1906 World Series. He got off to a poor start in 1907 and was forced to retire in mid-season. The career of the Iron Man of the Mound was suddenly over at age thirty-three, less than a year after his amazing pitching streak was ended.

John McGraw, the Player

ohn "Mugsy" McGraw is best remembered as the Hall of Fame manager of the New York Giants from 1902 to 1932. The axiom that star players make poor managers did not apply to McGraw, who as a player was the best third baseman in baseball during the 1890s.

The scrappy little infielder made his big-league debut in 1890 as an eighteen-year-old shortstop. By 1894, he was firmly entrenched as the star third baseman of the pennant-winning Baltimore Orioles. Young Mugsy hit .340 that year and was second in stolen bases with seventy-eight.

McGraw was a good base-stealer throughout his career, averaging sixty steals for every 150 games played. He was also a prolific run-scorer thanks to the guidance of Orioles manager Ned Hanlon, a big advocate of disciplined hitting. The five-foot-seven-inch McGraw became Hanlon's star pupil at drawing walks, and in 1898 he led the National League in walks with 112 and in runs scored.

JOHN J. McGRAW, Manager and Third Baseman
BALTIMORE, 1899.

The young John McGraw in 1899,

The next year, 1899, McGraw did even better and had the best year of his career. He hit .391, finishing third in the league in batting. Although limited to 117 games, he again led the league in walks, this time with 124, and in runs scored, with 140.

Sadly, an injury that year signaled the end of McGraw as a star player. He played only 117 games because of a serious spike wound to one of his knees. The injury was so severe that McGraw had a chronically dislocating knee for the rest of his playing career. He was just twenty-seven at the time, but he never again played as many as 100 games in a season. After 1901, he had only 195 at bats left in his career and hit a weak .251.

Fortunately, by that time McGraw had settled in as the brilliant, cantankerous, and colorful manager of the Giants. While the fans soon began to forget McGraw's fame as the fiery third-base star, old Mugsy was not above reminding them. He owned a pet margay, which is a small South American leopard, and often brought his pet out to the ballpark where it was the subject of much admiration. McGraw was fond of comparing the jungle cat to himself in his playing days—quick, calculating, and aggressive.

Baseball's Longest Game

T he rules say that an extra-inning game can go on for as long as the score remains tied and the conditions are playable. The longest game, by innings, in major-league history might still be going on if it hadn't been played before ballparks were lighted.

On May 1, 1920, no one was surprised when Joe Oeschger of the Boston Braves and Leon Cadore of the Brooklyn Dodgers hooked up in a brilliant pitcher's duel, headed for extra innings. Both pitchers were in their prime, and the last time they had faced each other they had taken a scoreless tie into extra innings before Cadore and the Dodgers won, 1-0.

Yet no one could have predicted the length of their struggle on this Saturday afternoon at Braves Field in Boston. Oeschger cracked first when he allowed a run in the top of the fourth, but the Braves bounced back to tie it with a run in the bottom of the fifth. Cadore, who worked as a magician in the off-season, went on to mesmerize the Dodger hitters for 20 consecutive shutout innings. And Oeschger matched him inning for inning.

Joe had pitched a twenty-inning game in 1919 and wasn't looking forward to doing it again. In the sixteenth inning he nearly ended it by hitting what looked to be a home run to left field, but Hall of Famer Zack Wheat made a leaping catch at the fence to keep the game alive.

In a 1980 interview, Oeschger recalled, "I was tired by the eighteenth inning, but the players kept telling me: 'Just one more inning, Joe, and we'll get a run.' " They never did.

The game, which had started at 3 p.m., finally was called because of darkness by umpire Barry McCormick. The score was still 1-1 and both pitchers were still on the mound. They had each pitched twenty-six innings in the longest game in major-league history.

Each side used only eleven players. Both leadoff men went to the plate eleven times. Surprisingly, the game lasted only 3 hours, 50 minutes. That's less than 1 hour, 20 minutes for each nine innings of baseball.

Oeschger explains that in those days pitchers worked quickly and they threw a lot of strikes because they were expected to finish the game. Joe estimated that he threw no more than 250 pitches that day, about 85 for every nine innings.

But 250 pitches is still an enormous number, and it is no surprise that Cadore never had a winning season after 1920. Oeschger, the only pitcher in history to twice work twenty innings in a single game, began to have arm trouble in 1922 and pitched very poorly until his early retirement at age thirty-three.

When the tie game was made up as part of a doubleheader in June, Joe Oeschger threw a three-hit shutout to settle the matter 1-0.

Baseball's Most Dramatic No-Hitter

Sam "Toothpick" Jones was a tall, right-handed pitcher who bounced around to a number of teams in his career from 1951 to 1964. He had an exceptional fastball, but he was also uncommonly wild. Three different times he led the league in *both* strikeouts and walks. In 1955 he actually allowed more walks than hits, 185 walks compared to just 175 hits.

Sam created a tough-guy image on the mound with a slovenly appearance which often included a shirttail only half tucked in and always featured a toothpick in his mouth—which led to his nickname of "Toothpick" Jones. In addition to the three strikeout titles and an ERA title in 1959, Toothpick is best remembered for his performance as a Chicago Cub on May 12, 1955.

Pitching at home against Pittsburgh, Jones went into the ninth inning with a 4-0 lead and a no-hitter on the line. Wrigley Field hadn't seen a no-hitter since the famous Toney-Vaughn double no-hit game thirty-eight years before in 1917. And Jones could notch another piece of immorality as the first black pitcher to throw a no-hitter in the major leagues.

Yet all of the hope turned into doubt as Jones suddenly suffered an attack of wildness. After the leadoff batter in the ninth fouled off the first pitch, Jones walked him on four straight pitches. On a 2-2 pitch to the second hitter, he wild-pitched the runner to second, then promptly walked the batter. That prompted Cubs manager Stan Hack to get his bullpen up and throwing. The next hitter was Tom Saffell, who would hit only .180 that year. Still, Jones could not find the plate, and on a 3-1 pitch loaded the bases.

Now, rather than worrying about the no-hitter, Jones had to fight to win the game. The bags were packed with the tying run at the plate, and he had yet to retire a batter! Hack went to the mound, but decided to ride out the storm with Sam. The vote of confidence seemed to turn Jones around as he whiffed Dick Groat on three straight pitches.

The next batter, Hall of Famer Roberto Clemente, swung fruitlessly at two pitches and fouled off two more before finally going down swinging. With two outs and a grand slam still capable of tying the game, Jones found himself facing cleanup hitter Frank Thomas, the Pirates' leader in home runs. With the count at 1-2, Sam caught Thomas looking for a strikeout to end the game.

Amazingly, "Toothpick" Jones had walked the bases full in a 4-0 game, then come back to strike out the side and seal his no-hitter. For the most amazing finish of any no-hitter in baseball history, Jones was presented with a gold toothpick.

Sam "Toothpick" Jones with Cleveland in 1952.

The Birth of Modern Baseball

B aseball evolved over time from several games. But if the modern game has a founder, it is Alexander Cartwright; if it has a first team, it is the Knickerbocker Club; and if it has a birthday, it is June 19. On that day in 1846, the first game was played under the "Cartwright rules" which later became known as the "Knickerbocker Rules."

The Knickerbocker Club was a gentlemen's athletic club in New York. One of its more active members was an adventuresome surveyor named Alexander Cartwright. It was he who first laid out the bases in a ninety-foot square. He was the first to settle on three outs to a side, nine men to a team, and nine innings to a game.

Ironically, in the first competitive game under their own rules, the Knicker-bockers were soundly defeated 23-1. The name of the victorious squad has not survived, and they are simply remembered as the New York Nine. After the Knickerbockers' lopsided loss, Cartwright's club decided to play just among them-selves for the rest of the decade.

Alexander Cartwright did not stay around to see his new game become a popular pastime on the East Coast. Nor was he around when the Civil War brought hundreds of thousands of young men together and then sent them home, with not only a knowledge of war but also a standardized version of baseball under the Knickerbocker Rules.

Cartwright left New York and went to California as part of the 1849 Gold Rush. He continued west to Hawaii, where he was involved in another of his life's passions. You see, Cartwright had joined the Knickerbocker Club because of its interest in firefighting. The name of the club was actually borrowed from a famous volunteer fire company. In Honolulu, Cartwright is not remembered as the father of baseball but as the founder of the fire department.

Back in New York, the Knickerbocker Club eventually became famous for its proficiency in baseball, and continued to be a force in the growth of the game under the Knickerbocker Rules. In 1858, the club took on a new member who proved to be an excellent player as well as another significant baseball pioneer. That man was Harry Wright, who eventually moved west and in 1866 organized the Cincinnati Red Stockings as baseball's first professional team.

The Tragic End
to Mickey Cochrane's Career

ickey Cochrane, known as "Black Mike" because of his raven-colored hair, was one of the most respected players in baseball during a career which stretched from 1925 to 1937. He was a tenacious competitor and a tremendous defensive catcher with remarkable durability. He was the first catcher to catch over 100 games in ten consecutive seasons, and he averaged 126 games behind the plate for the first eleven years of his career. Despite the physical demands of the position, he managed a .320 career batting average while hitting for above-average power. He was also the best-running catcher of his era.

Seven times in his eleven full seasons, he was recognized as the best catcher in baseball, and twice he was voted his league's Most Valuable Player. He played on

Mickey Cochrane

three consecutive pennant winners with the Philadelphia Athletics and, when the Depression forced Connie Mack to sell off his stars, the Detroit Tigers were fortunate enough to acquire the thirty-one-year-old Cochrane as their player-manager. Cochrane won the pennant his first two years on the job, but his career was suddenly derailed at age thirty-four.

Cochrane was off to a fine start in 1937. In late May he was hitting .306 and slugging just under .500. He had an on-base percentage of .447 and had scored an amazing 27 runs in 27 games played.

On May 25, he homered off Yankee pitcher Bump Hadley. The next time Mickey came up, Hadley delivered a fastball on a 3-1 count. The ball sailed up and in and struck Cochrane a couple of inches above his left eyebrow, knocking him cold.

When Cochrane was revived in the clubhouse, he asked that the game be held up so he could return, then fell back into unconsciousness and hovered in a near-coma for ten days. X-rays showed his skull had been fractured in three places.

When Cochrane recovered, he showed great class in exonerating Hadley of intentionally beaning him after Mickey had homered in his last at bat. Cochrane admitted that with a man on first base he had been crowding the plate looking for a pitch he could pull behind the runner. Besides, Mickey pointed out, who would throw a beanball on 3-1 with first base already occupied?

Despite a recovery to full health, the damage to Cochrane's skull left him extremely vulnerable to more serious injury. The doctors warned that a second blow to the head could kill him. Cochrane never played another game, a tragically premature ending for one of baseball's greatest catchers.

Doc Parker's Last Stand

arley "Doc" Parker was a husky right-handed pitcher and utility man who played with the Chicago Cubs in the 1890s. Actually, he did a bit of everything, also serving as the team trainer and primary batting-practice pitcher. He rarely pitched in a scheduled game, and when the Cubs released him after the 1896 season he had only five career wins against seven losses and an ERA of 5.27.

Parker appeared to vanish from the majors, but in 1899 the Pirates gave a brief tryout to a pitcher named Jay Parker who claimed to be Doc Parker's brother. That was a rather suspicious claim. When Jay Parker was questioned about his age, he gave a birthdate that was less than a month after Doc Parker's. At the same time, they couldn't deny that he pitched like his brother. Jay Parker made one appearance and didn't get anyone out. He retired with a career ERA of infinity.

In 1901, five years after Doc Parker was last seen in the majors, he surfaced again in an attempt to help the beleaguered Cincinnati Reds, who were struggling in seventh place. This version of Doc—or Jay or whoever this Parker was—somehow talked his way into starting against the Brooklyn Dodgers on June 21.

The Reds left Parker in for the whole game and the result was a record-breaking massacre. Doc Parker had absolutely nothing in his 1901 comeback. The best thing that could be said about his performance was that he walked only two men—everyone else was too busy getting hits. Parker gave up a homer, five doubles, and twenty singles, and didn't strike out a batter. Brooklyn scored in every inning as they piled up 21 runs.

It could have been even worse. If the game had been played in Cincinnati rather than Brooklyn, Parker probably would have pitched a ninth inning.

As it was, Doc Parker did more than enough damage to keep his name in the record book. He still holds the National League record for runs given up in a game, and the major-league record for most hits allowed in a game.

Doc was released the next day and neither he—nor brother Jay—ever pitched again in the major leagues.

Stan Musial—Pitcher?

The St. Louis Cardinals have produced several Hall of Famers, but only one has been called "baseball's most perfect warrior." Stan "The Man" Musial was the model superstar with a career of awesome, consistent brilliance.

Musial broke into the majors by batting .426 in a late-season call-up in 1941, which began a streak of seventeen consecutive seasons during which he batted .310 or higher. He won seven batting titles, the last at age thirty-six. In 1962, when Stan was a forty-one-year-old grandfather, he turned in a .330 batting average.

His career average of .331 is second in his era only to Ted Williams, but the left-handed outfielder-first baseman was far from just a high-average hitter. He was known for his ability to slash line drives off the boards in old Sportsman's Park. Although he never took a home run crown, he led the league eight times in doubles and five times in triples. He also had six seasons of 30 or more home runs and totaled 475 home runs in his career.

Stan played all of his twenty-two years with the Cardinals. He played on four pennant winners, and three times was honored as the league's Most Valuable Player. Oddly enough, it took a little bad luck to get this great hitting career started.

You see, Musial first signed with the Cardinals as a seventeen-year-old left-handed pitcher. At age eighteen he pitched for the first-place club in the Mountain State League and went 9-2 with the league's tenth-best ERA. The fact that he also hit .352 was easily overlooked, as he had only 71 at bats and was playing in a hitter's league where his whole team had averaged .306.

The next year, 1940, Musial was promoted to the Florida State League and had an even more impressive season on the mound. Musial doubled his wins and led the league in winning percentage as he won eighteen games and lost only five. In 223 innings he had an ERA of 2.62. That season he also played his first games as a professional outfielder, batting .311 as an outfielder between starts on the mound.

At that point in his minor-league career, Musial had averaged .310 in 538 at bats, but had hit only three home runs. He had been far more successful on the mound and likely would have remained there if an injury hadn't ended his pitching career.

Late in the 1940 season, Musial went after a fly ball and slipped and fell heavily on his throwing arm. It irritated an old injury he had suffered in a gymnastics workout and his career as a pitcher was over. Concentrating solely on his hitting, Musial proved to be a marvelously quick study. The next year he hit .379 and led the West Virginia League with 26 homers. By September he was in the majors—and the rest is baseball history.

Stan Musial pitching in the minors.

The Greatest Strikeout Performance Ever

Ron Necciai began his career as a first baseman in the Pittsburgh Pirates' organization, but after watching him throw they quickly moved the tall right-hander to the pitcher's mound. His lack of control was an immediate problem, and in 1951 he lost his first seven starts while pitching in the lowly Class D North Carolina League. But Ron finished the season well and, based strictly on ability, Pittsburgh wanted to jump him up to Class AA in 1952. But to build up Necciai's confidence they decided to start him off in Class D again, this time with the Bristol Twins.

In his first start at Bristol, Necciai struck out twenty batters. In his next outing he whiffed nineteen. A few nights later his club was in a jam, facing the bases loaded and nobody out. Necciai came on in relief to strike out the side and went on to whiff eleven in a row as he pitched four perfect innings.

But nothing he had ever done before or since could compare with his next appearance. On May 13, 1942, he started against the Welch Miners of the Appalachian League and threw a no-hitter in which he walked only one batter and hit another. What made the game stand out from all other no-hitters was the fact that Rocket Ron Necciai struck out *twenty-seven* men.

That night, only two batters were able to hit a ball into fair territory against Rocket Ron. Both hit weak grounders; one was bobbled for an error by the shortstop, who probably had forgotten what the ball felt like. Necciai got the chance at the twenty-seventh strikeout when a swinging strike three got past the catcher and the batter made it safely to first.

After his historic outing, Ron struck out eight batters in a relief appearance. Then, in his final start with Bristol, Necciai said goodbye to the Appalachian League with a two-hitter, striking out twenty-four.

With results like those, there was no way Necciai could remain in Class D. he was averaging an incredible twenty-three strikeouts per nine innings. So Rocket Ron was promoted in mid-season to Burlington, the Pirates' Class B team. The results there were almost as impressive. He struck out 172 batters in just 126 innings while posting a 1.57 ERA. There was talk of bringing him up to the majors, and in August he was told to report to Pittsburgh.

It was an amazing journey for the former first baseman who had started off losing his first seven games. Now, in a single season, he had jumped from the absolute bottom of professional baseball to the pinnacle of the major leagues. But here the magic ended. In fifty-five innings with the Pirates Rocket Ron struck out only thirty-one men and walked thirty-two. He had a 7.04 ERA and lost seven games against a single victory.

That was Ron Necciai's one shot at the majors. The next year he started off in the minors, and a combination of ulcers and arm trouble kept him there until 1959 when he retired at age twenty-seven. It was a sad ending for the minor-league legend who struck out twenty-seven batters in a single game.

Baseball's Oldest Single-Season Batting Record

wen "Chief" Wilson, a right fielder with the Pittsburgh Pirates, was not a likely candidate to set any lasting records. He played only nine seasons in the majors and had a mediocre career batting average of .269.

The only thing that made Wilson stand out on a baseball field was his size. During his career from 1908 to 1916, the average batter was just under five-feet-eleven. At six-feet-two, Wilson was the Pirates' largest player and usually led the club in homers and little else.

He never led the league in any offensive category until his strange season in 1912

Owen "Chief" Wilson

when triples began flying off his bat in record numbers. When the dust settled, the record books showed he had legged out an unbelievable thirty-six triples.

Generally, triples are associated with fast players, which made Wilson's feat that much stranger. By all accounts, Wilson was not an exceptionally fast runner, nor does his playing record suggest such speed. In an era in which base stealing was an important part of the game, he never stole more than seventeen bases in a season.

The only indication that he was capable of producing triples in bunches had come the season before. On July 24, 1911, Wilson tied the record for this century by collecting three triples in a single game. But he still finished the season with only twelve triples, and his highest total after his thirty-six-triple season was only fourteen. What happened with Chief Wilson in 1912 was like a steady twenty-homer man suddenly hitting sixty homers and then never coming close again.

When Chief Wilson passed away in 1954, every significant offensive record had been broken at least once since his fateful 1912 season. Since his death, we have seen a new home run record in 1961, and the record for stolen bases has been broken three times. But no one has come even remotely close to Wilson's thirty-six triples.

The next-highest season total in all of baseball history is a distant twenty-six triples. No seasonal batting record can match that 28 percent gap between first and second place. We are far more likely to see another .400-hitter or sixty-homer season before anyone even approaches a thirty-triple season. The chances of a player actually challenging Wilson's total of 36 three-baggers borders on zero. This is one entry in the record book that seems etched in stone.

The Birth of the Spitball

hen baseball entered the twentieth century, several pitchers had learned they could give their pitches extra life by scuffing or cutting the ball. But intentionally damaging the ball was against the rules and frowned upon by the umpires. The spitball was a unique innovation because it gave the pitchers a chance to openly alter the flight of the pitch without shortening the life of the baseball.

There are several claims to the origin of the spitball, but there is only one trail that led to its establishment in the big leagues. It began with a harmless game of catch on a rainy day in 1901. Eastern League outfielder George Hildebrand was warming up with pitcher "Fiddler" Corridon when Hildebrand begin to lose his grip on the wet ball. The ball slipped out of his hand and suddenly dove downward just as it reached his target.

Intrigued by this unusual motion, Hildebrand tried to duplicate his throw using spit on the ball rather than dew. Eventually he was able to throw a consistent wet sinker and the spitball was born. Hildebrand and Corridon continued to refine the pitch, and Corridon went on to use the pitch in the major leagues.

If it had been up to Corridon, his secret weapon would have died with him, but Hildebrand enjoyed teaching the pitch to anyone who was interested. His most significant pupil was Elmer Stricklett, a small right-hander looking for some edge to get him to the big leagues. After learning Hildebrand's spitball, Elmer won eleven games in a row and was sold to the White Sox in 1904.

Sox manager Fielder Jones was impressed with Stricklett's spitter and asked him to teach the pitch to the rookie pitcher assigned as his roommate. That twenty-three-year-old rookie was Big Ed Walsh.

Stricklett taught the pitch to Walsh, but for a while Big Ed had a difficult time controlling the pitch and used it only as a novelty on the sidelines. Finally, in 1906, Walsh felt sufficiently confident to use the pitch in a game. He promptly won seven games in a row and immediately went from a mediocrity to one of the best pitchers in his era and the greatest spitballer in baseball history.

Walsh's success caused the pitch to spread like wildfire throughout the majors and all of professional baseball. It remained entrenched until 1920 when it was outlawed for any pitcher not already established as a major league spitballer. Burleigh Grimes threw the last legal spitball in 1934. It was a long ride for a pitch that began thirty-three years earlier with an outfielder throwing on a rainy day.

Oscar Charleston, Star Center Fielder of the Old Negro Leagues

While Satchel Paige was the biggest drawing card of the Negro Leagues, and Josh Gibson was considered the greatest hitter, Oscar Charleston was the league's greatest all-around player—and perhaps the greatest of all time in any league.

The only problem in presenting his credentials is deciding where to begin. Some claim that in his prime Charleston was as fast as the legendary Cool Papa Bell. He began his athletic career as a track star for a black outfit in the United States Army. They called him "The Hoosier Comet," and when he entered professional baseball he quickly established himself as one of the league's best base stealers.

Because he was a center fielder and great base stealer, when Charleston led his league with a .430 batting average in 1925, it was only natural for the newspapers to

Oscar Charleston, the "Black Ty Cobb."

refer to him as "The Black Ty Cobb." But Oscar was a great power hitter and took the home run crown to go with his batting title.

Charleston was also a much better defensive center fielder than Ty Cobb. In the field they called Oscar "The Greyhound of the Garden" and compared him to Hall of Famer Tris Speaker. He was especially well-known for his acrobatic fielding in exhibition games. On certain flyballs he would come charging in, do a flying forward flip, and land on his feet to make the catch. Take that, Ozzie Smith!

Charleston was born too soon to get the chance to play in the majors, but few witnesses will ever forget his performance against the St. Louis Cardinals in 1921. At that time Oscar was a member of the St. Louis Giants in the Negro League. At the end of the season, the major-league Cardinals agreed to play the black team in a five-game exhibition. It was the first time the twenty-four-year-old Charleston played against major leaguers.

The Cardinals were coming off a strong year in which they had finished twenty-one games over .500, and Hall of Famer Rogers Hornsby had taken the batting title with a .397 average. But the star of the exhibition series was clearly Charleston. In one game, Oscar belted *four* homers, including two off Hall of Fame pitcher Jesse "Pop" Haines. To put the feat in perspective, it would be another eleven years before Lou Gehrig would become the first major leaguer in this century to hit four homers in a single game.

Oscar Charleston was inducted into the Hall of Fame in 1976. Few have deserved the honor more.

The Wildest Triple Play in History

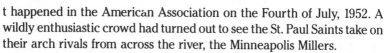

t happened in the American Association on the Fourth of July, 1952. A wildly enthusiastic crowd had turned out to see the St. Paul Saints take on their arch rivals from across the river, the Minneapolis Millers.

In the third inning, St. Paul had a solid rally going. They had scored one run and their star hitter, Bob Wilson, was at the plate with the bases loaded and nobody out.

Wilson hit a long fly to center fielder Bob Lennon for an apparent sacrifice. The runner from third beat Lennon's throw to the plate. Catcher Ray Katt made a snap throw back to second to nab Sandy Amoros, who was making a belated attempt to advance from first base on the throw.

The Millers then threw on to third base in hopes of catching Jack Cassini, the runner from second who had advanced to third and aggressively rounded the bag too far. Unfortunately, the second baseman's throw was wild and Cassini scampered home with what looked like the second run.

Where did the third out come from? The Millers picked up a delayed triple play when their Hall of Fame third baseman Ray Dandridge retrieved the wild throw and stepped on third, claiming that Pat McGlothin, the original runner on third, had left too early on the fly to center. The umpires upheld the appeal and bedlam reigned as they tried to figure out whether or not a run had scored.

Obviously McGlothlin's run did not count, but the umpires ruled correctly that the second run was legitimate because it had scored on a wild throw before the appeal was made. The Millers used their big play to send the Saints home with a 5-2 loss, but the Saint's fans could console themselves with the knowledge that they had witnessed baseball's wildest triple play.

Think about it. The Millers pulled off a triple play in which they retired both the batter and the lead runner, but still allowed a run to score. It remains one of a kind in both minor- and major-league history.

William "Dummy" Hoy's Battle to Become a Winner

hen Willie Hoy graduated with highest honors as the class valedictorian from the School for the Deaf in Columbus, Ohio, he was only fifteen years old and dreaming of a career as a professional ballplayer.

Although he was totally deaf, he eventually got the chance to play professionally with Oshkosh in the North West League. In 1888, when he was twenty-five, the last-place Washington Nationals brought him to the major leagues.

Hoy was not an imposing figure, standing only five-feet-four and weighing just 150 pounds, but he was an excellent defensive outfielder with plenty of speed and a strong arm. At the plate he made a good leadoff man because of his excellent eye and ability as a base stealer.

In his rookie season, he led the National League in steals and was second in drawing walks. To keep up with the ball/strike count, he persuaded the umpires to raise their right arm whenever a pitch was a strike. This proved to be a boon to the crowd as well, since they often could not hear the umpire's call, and it became a standard at all ballgames.

Hoy wasn't bothered by his nickname of "Dummy," which referred to his deafness, but he desperately wanted to prove himself as a winning player. He was eager to escape last-place Washington when the Players League formed in 1890, but the only team willing to take a chance in him was Buffalo, the team destined to be the doormat of the new league.

When that league folded, Hoy was determined not to return to the ragtag Washington club, and Charlie Comiskey agreed to give him a trial with his St. Louis Browns in the American Association. It was Hoy's first experience on a team that wasn't destined for last place. The club finished a strong second as Hoy led the league in walks with 119 and led the team with 136 runs scored.

But then the American Association folded and Hoy had to either return to Washington or give up major-league baseball. After Hoy had put in two more seasons with the hapless Washington Nationals, his old buddy Charlie Comiskey— then managing the Cincinnati Reds—traded for Hoy. In 1897 the Reds finished

William "Dummy" Hoy with the Washington Nationals in 1888.

twenty games over .500 as Hoy hit .292 and was recognized as the league's best defensive outfielder.

But when Comiskey left the Reds, Hoy quickly found himself traded to Louisville, another perennial loser. Hoy played well there; he hit .318 and then .306, and set an all-time record by throwing out three runners at the plate in one game.

Then, while at the top of his game, Dummy Hoy vanished from the scene. To find him, you had to look for Charlie Comiskey, the first man to believe in Dummy Hoy as a winning ballplayer. Comiskey had bought the Chicago franchise in the newly formed American League. When the White Sox won the league's first major-league pennant in 1901, out in center field was a .294 hitter who had led the league in walks and scored 112 runs. It was thirty-nine-year-old Dummy Hoy, a winner at last.

Ernie Banks the Shortstop

Ernie Banks, the man known as Mr. Cub, is listed with the first basemen in baseball's Hall of Fame because he played more games there than at any other position. But he made the Hall more on the basis of his accomplishments as a shortstop, the position he played during his first nine seasons. He played over 1,100 games at shortstop—only 134 games less than at first base.

Ernie joined the Cubs in 1953 as a shortstop from the dying Negro Leagues. The tall, rangy twenty-two-year-old became the Cubs' regular shortstop the next year and surprised folks by hitting 19 home runs. But they hadn't seen anything yet. The next year he belted 44 home runs, a new major-league record for shortstops.

In 1958, he broke his own record by belting 47 homers. He also hit .313 and led the league with 129 RBIs to win the league's Most Valuable Player award. The next year he won again, the first player in National League history to win back-to-back MVP awards. This time he hit 45 homers with a league-leading 143 RBIs. He also led the league's shortstops with 519 assists and a .985 fielding percentage.

The next year, Banks just missed a third MVP award as he led the league with 41 homers and had his best year ever in the field. Ernie led in virtually everything—most putouts, most assists, most double plays, highest fielding percentage—and he was honored with the Gold Glove award for defensive excellence.

In 1961, Ernie Banks' career as a shortstop came to an abrupt end at age thirty. He suffered a knee injury which ended a streak of 717 consecutive games played, all of them at shortstop. In 1962, the ailing knee forced Banks to move full-time to first base, and he never played shortstop again in his remaining ten seasons.

The bum knee also hurt Ernie's hitting. In those last ten years he averaged only .258 with 24 homers and 89 RBIs for every 150 games played. Those figures were a far cry from his amazing performance while at shortstop. In his nine years at shortstop, his batting average was .290, and for every 150 games played he averaged *37* homers and *106* RBIs.

It is Banks' power hitting that will never be forgotten. Despite playing his last game at shortstop at age thirty, Banks still has 80 more career home runs as a shortstop than anyone else in baseball history. Of the eight seasons in which a shortstop has hit more than 30 homers, Banks has six of them, including the top *five!* No other player in baseball history has so completely dominated the power statistics at one position as Ernie Banks—baseball's most powerful shortstop.

Seasons by a Shortstop with Over 30 Home Runs	
1) 47, Ernie Banks 1958	5) 41, Ernie Banks 1960
2) 45, Ernie Banks 1959	6) 40, Rico Petrocelli 1969
3) 44, Ernie Banks 1955	7) 39, Vern Stephens 1949
4) 43, Ernie Banks 1957	8) 37, Ernie Banks 1962

Ebenezer Beatin,
Baseball's First False Hero

Every few years, a young player makes the big leagues after a tremendous build-up and then proves to be a total flop. One of the earliest such cases was Ebenezer Ambrose Beatin.

According to baseball researcher Jim Baker, in 1886 this nineteen-year-old right-handed pitcher was one of the most prized talents in the country. He had won so many amateur games for the Allentown baseball team that he became known as the "Allentown Wonder."

The simple proof of the enthusiasm for his talents is that Ebenezer signed contracts for the 1887 season with *five* different clubs, including three in the National League alone. When the legal mess as sorted out, the overjoyed winner of Beatin's services was the Detroit Wolverines.

Ebenezer Beatin
in 1889 with the
Cleveland Spiders.

However, the bloom quickly faded from this rose. Although the Wolverines were one of the best teams in the National League, Beatin had a losing record in his two seasons with the club before being traded to the Cleveland Spiders in 1889. In 1890, he led the league in losses with 31 and in hits allowed with *518* (he had thrown 474 innings). The next year he lost his first three decisions and, at age twenty-four, the "Allentown Wonder" was released, never to pitch in the big leagues again.

But the story of Ebenezer Beatin was connected to another pitcher's path to baseball's Hall of Fame. In Beatin's last full season with the Cleveland Spiders, the club acquired a young pitcher from the minor-league club in Canton, Ohio. Known as the Canton Cyclone, the youngster arrived with little fanfare as the purchase price was only $250 and a suit of clothes for the Canton club owner.

While Beatin lost 31 games as the club's number-one starter, the rookie pitcher quietly won 9 games against 7 defeats. When Beatin faltered in 1891, the Canton Cyclone took over his spot in the starting rotation and led the team with 27 victories. The youngster was just warming up as he went on to register another *475* major-league victories in a twenty-two-year period.

The future once predicted for Ebenezer Beatin came true for his successor. The Canton Cyclone was Denton True Young, the man for whom the Cy Young award is named and the winner of 511 major-league games.

The Original
Hall of Fame Game

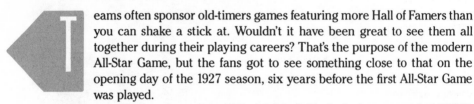

eams often sponsor old-timers games featuring more Hall of Famers than you can shake a stick at. Wouldn't it have been great to see them all together during their playing careers? That's the purpose of the modern All-Star Game, but the fans got to see something close to that on the opening day of the 1927 season, six years before the first All-Star Game was played.

That day the Yankees hosted the Philadelphia Athletics before a crowd of 72,000 fans and beat the A's 8-3. In retrospect, it was a game to remember, as it was the first time two clubs had played each other with no less than fourteen Hall of Famers decorating their rosters.

The Yankees had Babe Ruth, Lou Gehrig, center fielder Earle Combs, and pitchers Waite Hoyt and Herb Pennock. Among the Philadelphia Athletics were Jimmie Foxx, Al Simmons, Mickey Cochrane, Lefty Grove, Ty Cobb, Eddie Collins, and Zack Wheat. And the managers of both clubs, Miller Huggins of the Yankees and Connie Mack of the Athletics, were Hall of Fame managers.

It isn't much of a surprise that those two teams finished first and second, winning 201 games between them. Although the A's had more Hall of Famers, the Yankees had more star players in their prime and went on to become the World Champions.

Incredibly, the two teams set a new record for Hall of Famers when they got together the next year. In 1928, the Philadelphia Athletics released Zack Wheat, who was forty-two years old, but they picked up Hall of Famer Tris Speaker, who was looking to play one last season.

The Yankees held on to all of their Hall of Famers from 1927, and picked up two more in veteran spitballer Stan Coveleski and rookie catcher Bill Dickey. That created a gathering of *sixteen* Hall of Famers, a record that still stands today.

As they did in 1927, the two teams finished first and second in the pennant race. Take note, baseball general managers. It's a rather simplistic theory, but packing your roster with a lot of Hall of Fame players is one way to win a lot of games.

Lefty Grove's Super Season
—and His Most Disappointing Loss

In August 23, 1931, Hall of Fame pitcher Lefty Grove was a solid bet to become the first pitcher in American League history to win seventeen consecutive games. Grove was in the midst of his finest season. He had already won 25 games and lost only twice. His opponents for the day were the lowly St. Louis Browns, a team so bad they were already 35½ games behind Grove's Philadelphia Athletics, who were battling for their third straight pennant.

The two teams were scheduled for a Sunday doubleheader and the Browns chose to open with a right-hander named Dickie Coffman, a pitcher they had asked waivers on just three weeks earlier. Missing from the Athletics' lineup was left fielder Al Simmons who had an infected toe and received permission to go home for a few days.

Grove pitched his normally brilliant game, but with a man on first, rookie Jimmy Moore—who was replacing Simmons in left field—badly misjudged a line drive that sailed over his head to score the runner. Making matters worse, Philadelphia was shut out for the *first* time that season. Dickie Coffman pitched the game of his life, a three-hit shut out to win the game.

The impossible had happened. The St. Louis Browns had ended Grove's consecutive-win streak behind a pitcher who was coming off a season of 8-18 with a 5.14 ERA. Grove had thrown a "technical" shutout to lose the game 1-0 on an unearned run.

Lefty was known for his fierce temper, and he never took a loss harder than this one. While the club played the second game of the doubleheader—which the Athletics won 10-0—Grove went berserk in the visiting clubhouse. He tried to rip the clubhouse door off the hinges. He tore off his uniform and stomped on it. He threw everything he got his hands on, splintered wooden locker panels, and tried to pull out a shower head. Grove refused to talk to the press or anyone else for several days, and he never did forgive Al Simmons for taking the day off and setting up the rookie mistake that ended his win streak.

As it was, Grove's 1931 season was possibly the greatest for any pitcher in baseball history. His league-leading ERA of 2.06 took place in one of the heaviest-hitting eras

Lefty Grove in 1941. He has just lost in extra innings (on an error) while attempting to win his 300th game.

in baseball. Grove's 1931 ERA was 2.32 runs *below* the league average, and that remains the American League record.

Grove won 31 games and lost only 4. He could easily have gone through the season with just one defeat. Three of his four losses were by a single run despite strong pitching performances—4-3, 2-1, and the infamous 1-0 loss on an unearned run.

If it's any comfort to Grove in his remarkable near miss, the consecutive-win record that he shares with Walter Johnson and Smokey Joe Wood has never been broken. Given the circumstances of his loss, it only seems right.

Which Elmer Smith?

lmer John Smith of Sandusky, Ohio, had a difficult time making a name for himself in the big leagues. The problem was that folks tended to confuse him with another Elmer Smith, no relation, who had played fourteen seasons in the majors just thirteen years earlier.

The similarities were uncanny. The two Elmer Smiths had similar builds (five-feet-eleven, 175 pounds and five-feet-ten, 168), both were left-handed hitters, and both were outfielders playing usually in left or right field. They even played a good portion of their careers in the same state.

The original Elmer Smith began his career in Cincinnati where he played seven seasons after being traded away and back again. This pattern was repeated in northern Ohio with the second Elmer Smith. He began with the Cleveland Indians, and he too played seven seasons there after being traded away and back again. For good measure, he finished his career with a season in Cincinnati, the old stomping grounds of the original Elmer Smith.

The new Elmer Smith thought he had ended the confusion in 1920 by becoming a star platoon player with the World Champion Indians. Yet this only blurred the distinctions between the two. You see, he hit .316, which is pretty close to the .311 career average of the original Elmer Smith. And he drove in a career-high 103 runs—which happens to be the exact career high for RBIs by the original Elmer.

You see the problem? If you asked a baseball historian about a left-handed outfielder name Elmer Smith who once drove in a career-high 103 RBIs, he would ask if you meant the one who did it in 1893 or in 1920.

Fortunately, Elmer John Smith accomplished something in the 1920 World Series that distinguishes his playing record from all Elmer Smiths, both past and future. In the fifth game of the Series, facing Hall of Famer Burleigh Grimes with the bases loaded, Smith hit a grand-slam homer to give the Indians the lead in the game and in the Series.

Elmer John Smith has been known forever after as the first player to hit a grand slam in the World Series. And there the confusion of Elmer Smiths ends.

Minor-League Teenager
Strikes Out Ruth and Gehrig

ackie Mitchell was only seventeen when signed by the Chattanooga Lookouts in the Southern Association. As a youngster, Jackie had learned to pitch from a neighbor, who just happened to be Hall of Fame pitcher Dazzy Vance. Jackie was a slightly built left-hander who weighed only 130 pounds but had a good side-arm sinker that was tough on left-handed batters. On April 2, prior to the start of the 1931 season, the Chattanooga team played an exhibition game with the New York Yankees.

In the top of the first inning, the Yankees put two men on base. With the two lefties Ruth and Gehrig coming up, manager Bert Niehoff pulled his starter and brought in the young lefty.

1931 was the season in which Ruth and Gehrig would tie for the home run crown with 46 homers apiece, while Ruth hit .373 and Gehrig hit .341. But Mitchell was up to the task. The seventeen-year-old caught the Babe looking at a 1-2 sinker for strike three. And to the amazement of the fans, Jackie retired the Iron Horse on three straight *swinging* strikes.

Tony Lazzeri ended the string by drawing a walk and Jackie was removed from the game. The Yankees went on to win the contest 14-4, but young Jackie Mitchell

Lou Gehrig and Babe Ruth watch as 17-year-old Jackie Mitchell warms up. (From the collection of Wayne Stivers.)

was the story of the game. Unfortunately, Mitchell's career ended shortly thereafter. The youngster's contract was disallowed by Baseball Commissioner Kenesaw Mountain Landis, who charged that Chattanooga's owner Joe Engel was signing Mitchell solely as a promotional gimmick, and thus it was not in the game's best interest. You see, Jackie Mitchell was a girl.

Were the strikeouts of Ruth and Gehrig a put-on? Well, that point remains unclear. There was no arrangement with the umpire nor was there a pre-arranged agreement with Ruth and Gehrig that they would strike out, although they were asked not to hit the ball up the middle.

Yet it did appear that both of the Yankee sluggers were giving less than their best. After his called strike three, Ruth slammed down his bat and stormed back to the dugout in what appeared to be theatrical mock anger. After Gehrig went down swinging on three strikes, he openly laughed on his way back to the bench.

Whatever the case, Jackie was a successful pitcher in a man's game. The Chattanooga team had first taken an interest in her when she had struck out nine men in a row in a local contest. She completely overwhelmed the opposition when forced to play in a women's league, and in 1932 she returned to play in the men's leagues. One story has her pitching part-time with Greensboro in the Piedmont League, the lowest rung of the minor leagues. She later barnstormed with the famous House of David baseball team before retiring in 1937. And no matter what the circumstances, Jackie Mitchell remains a baseball legend as the woman who struck out Babe Ruth and Lou Gehrig.

Baseball's Oddest Trades

Your typical baseball trade routinely involves the transfer of money and players. But in the old days of the independent minor leagues, cash flow was often a problem. Deals would take place under a barter system that allowed a player to be swapped for just about anything from mules to buses to a fresh coat of paint at the ballpark.

Joe Engel, the maverick owner of the Chattanooga Lookouts, once traded shortstop Johnny Johns for a turkey—not a bad ballplayer, but a real turkey, feathers and all!

Joe Martina, a long-time pitching star in the Texas League, started off as "Iron-man" Martina, but then his Dallas club traded him to his hometown of New Orleans. In return they got two barrels of oysters. From then on, he was always known as "Oyster Joe."

Big names found themselves involved in some of these bizarre minor-league deals. In 1890, Cy Young was shipped from Canton, Ohio, to Cleveland for $250 and a suit of clothes. In 1920, Baltimore of the International League worked out a deal in which they built a new outfield fence for the team in Martinsburg, West Virginia. In return they got Martinsburg's star pitcher, who happened to be Lefty Grove.

That same year there was a major-league deal that rivaled the unusual barter system of the old minor leagues, and involved the most popular ballplayer in baseball history. The sale of Babe Ruth from Boston to New York in 1920 was highly unorthodox if not illegal.

The Yankees officially agreed to pay $100,000 for Ruth's contract, but more important to Red Sox owner Harry Frazee was a loan of $300,000 from Jake Ruppert, co-owner of the Yankees. Frazee was trying to hold off bankruptcy in his main business of producing stage plays. There was no way the deal would have gone through without the loan.

But Ruppert was not going to loan the extra $300,000 without some form of security. The only thing that Frazee owned of significant value was Fenway Park. Although it was totally unethical and certainly would not be allowed today, the New York Yankees held a mortgage on the home field of the Boston Red Sox for nearly five years until Frazee struck it rich on his investment in the popular stage play *No, No, Nanette*. It remains part of the Babe Ruth legend that he is the only player to be traded for a mortgage on a major-league park.

Satchel Paige's
Amazing Drawing Power

eing a rookie usually comes before being a legend, but Satchel Paige was a legend long before his rookie year in the majors. Paige was the biggest star the old Negro leagues ever had. Even baseball fans who knew nothing of the black leagues had heard of the legendary Satchel Paige. He was a mythic figure of the proportions of Babe Ruth. One of the popular mind-games of the fans was to ask, "What if Paige were allowed to play in the majors?" That "What if…" became a reality when Bill Veeck signed Paige to pitch for Cleveland in the middle of the 1948 pennant race, and the fans literally knocked down the gates to see Paige finally pitch in the major leagues.

Paige's first start was on the road in Chicago. The attendance was given as 51,000, a new record at the time for a night game in Comiskey Park. And that was just the paid attendance. When informed of the sellout, a large group of fans stormed one of the gates, actually uprooting a turnstile. Bill Veeck remembers that the aisles were packed with an illicit standing-room crowd. Estimates for the total crowd went as high as 70,000.

For his first three starts in the majors Paige drew 202,000 fans, an average of over 67,000. The crowds set attendance records of one form or another for Paige's first five starts. The biggest crowd was before the hometown fans on August 20. No less than 78,382 fans filled Cleveland's Municipal Stadium. That remains the largest nighttime crowd in baseball history. With baseball's number-one drawing card, Cleveland went on to set a new single-season attendance record and became the first team ever to draw over two million fans.

How did Satchel Paige do before these record crowds? There had been some concern over how much Satchel Paige had left in his golden arm. After all, Satchel was at least forty-two years old at the time. Cleveland manager Lou Boudreau was utterly opposed to Paige's signing until he actually hit against Satchel in a secret tryout.

The Indians used Paige primarily as a relief pitcher, but he was called on to make seven starts and pitched remarkably well. In those seven starts he won four, lost none, and threw two shutouts. One of those shutouts came before that record crowd of more than 78,000 fans. That was also the fourth shutout in a row for the Indians, to set a record which lasted twenty-six years.

Overall, Paige was 6-1 with a 2.48 ERA in a season when the league ERA was 4.28. It's fairly safe to say that the signing of Paige determined the pennant race as Cleveland edged Boston by a single win. Appropriately, Paige became the first black pitcher to appear in the World Series and was perfect in his one relief appearance.

Satchel Paige with
the Kansas City
Monarchs.

The Worst Pitcher
to Ever Throw a No-Hitter

I n May 6, 1953, Bobo Holloman was a bad relief pitcher working for a bad team, the St. Louis Browns. The Browns had already decided to send Holloman to the minors, but he was granted a courtesy start for one last chance to show his stuff. Somehow, in his first start in the major leagues, Bobo ended up throwing a no-hitter against the Philadelphia Athletics!

But this was not your run of the mill no-hitter. For starters, Bobo walked five batters, three in one inning, and was helped by several sensational fielding plays, including two key double plays.

In the second inning, the left fielder made a circus catch on an apparent double. The very next inning Holloman walked the leadoff man but gave up a screaming line drive right at the third baseman who turned it into a double play. In the eighth inning shortstop Billy Hunter made the play of the game, a tremendous diving stop followed by a powerful throw that just nipped the batter at first.

But it was more than good defense that made this no-hitter possible. There were also several apparent hits that just missed being fair balls. The A's Allie Clark hit one into the seats that went foul by only a couple of feet. Joe Astroth laid down a beauty of a bunt that kicked foul at the last second, and Eddie Robinson, the final batter of the game, smoked a line drive over the first baseman's head that landed foul by no more than a couple of inches. Eddie then flied out to end the game, and Bobo Holloman became a baseball immortal.

Bobo's no-hitter was full of oddities, not the least of which was that the last no-hitter by a St. Louis Brown had been thrown in 1934 by Louis Newsom—probably the only other pitcher in major-league history with the nickname of "Bobo."

Holloman's performance left the Browns in a quandary. They knew his no-hitter had been more luck than ability, but how could they now go ahead with their plans to send him to the minors? For the sake of the fans they had to leave Bobo in the rotation and hope his luck would hold.

It didn't. Bobo lasted only two innings in his next start. He made nine more starts and his no-hitter remained the only complete game of his career. He finished the season with an ERA of 5.21 and never pitched again in the majors. Going by his career statistics, he is easily the worst pitcher in major-league history to ever record a no-hitter.

The Story of
Mordecai "Three Finger" Brown

ordecai Centennial Brown was given his middle name because he was born in 1876, the hundredth year of the Republic, but he picked up an even more unusual nickname from a childhood accident. When he was seven years old Mordecai caught his right hand in his uncle's corn grinder, lost most of his forefinger, and mangled his middle finger.

Brown still went on to become a professional ballplayer, but started as a third baseman before discovering his mangled hand could give him an edge as a pitcher. He found that placing the stub of his forefinger on the ball gave a sharp downward break to his curveball. Within two years he was in the majors, and he enjoyed a fourteen-year career (1903-16) as one of the best pitchers in the big leagues.

Pitching with the Chicago Cubs, he had a streak of six straight twenty-win seasons and a winning percentage over .730. He had four straight seasons from

Mordecai "Three Finger" Brown with the Chicago Cubs.

1906 through 1909 in which all his ERAs were under 1.50! In 1906, he set a record for the lowest ERA by a pitcher with over 250 innings. Brown thew shutouts in nearly a third of his starts (10 of 32) and finished with an ERA of 1.04!

Brown was the key pitcher during the Cubs' dynasty, when they won four pennants in five years (1906-10). When they finished second in 1909, Brown still led the league with 27 wins and had an ERA of 1.31, pitching a league-leading 343 innings.

One of Brown's strengths as a pitcher was his versatility. He was known for having an unbelievably "loose" arm and frequently pitched as a reliever between starts. He never bothered to warm up in such cases but would just head to the mound, take eight warm-up tosses, and be ready to go.

In 1911, Brown collected thirteen saves, which made him the first pitcher in baseball history to reach double figures in that category. While he was a consistent twenty-game winner, Brown led the league in saves four straight years and in relief wins twice. The most critical win of Brown's career actually came in a relief appearance. In 1908, the Cubs and Giants had to play a one-game playoff to decide the pennant. When the Giants quickly scored a run in the first, Brown entered the game in relief and allowed only four hits in eight innings as he won the game and the pennant 4-2.

Brown retired at age forty to operate a garage in his hometown of Terre Haute, Indiana. He often gave directions to his uncle's farm, where they had polished and put on display the feed grinder that launched the sensational career of Mordecai "Three-Finger" Brown.

The Highest-Scoring Game
in Professional Baseball History

The famous 51-3 game between Corsicana and Texarkana in the 1902 Texas League remains the largest run total by one club, as well as the largest winning margin in baseball history. But their record combined total of 54 runs was soundly broken thirty years later.

It happened on April 6, 1932, in the first professional baseball game ever played in Albuquerque, New Mexico. The Albuquerque Dons were a new entry in the Arizona-Texas League, and were hosting the El Paso Longhorns at Tingly Field, the Dons' home park.

In spite of less-than-ideal weather, a large crowd came out for the afternoon game. Things looked pretty glum for the hometown fans as the visiting Longhorns scored seven runs in their first at bats, but the Dons answered the challenge with eight runs in the bottom of the first. This clearly was not going to be a normal game.

In the end, Albuquerque fans were introduced to professional baseball by a game that featured a record 58 runs. They probably enjoyed it, as their boys scored 43 of them.

If there was an explanation for this offensive outburst, it could probably be found in the weather. When the Albuquerque Dons beat the El Paso Longhorns 43-15, they were near a ferocious storm front and their game was played in winds that reportedly gusted to 55 to 65 miles an hour.

Because the wind was blowing in from right center, there was only one home run among the 58 runs scored. But any ball hit into the air was a wild adventure, and it was nearly impossible to throw the ball with any accuracy. The game featured fourteen triples and twelve errors, most of which were throwing errors.

The pitchers didn't fare much better. They issued a total of twenty-one walks and hit five batters. There were actually fewer hits than runs. But probably the most remarkable statistic in the boxscore from this incredible game is that it was completed in just 2 hours, 40 minutes. That's an average of one run every 2 minutes, 45 seconds—probably one more record from Albuquerque's first professional baseball game.

The Mysterious Decline of Chuck Klein

o player in baseball history had a better start to his big-league career than Philadelphia Phillies star Chuck Klein. In his first five full seasons he looked like a combination of Ty Cobb and Babe Ruth.

Five consecutive seasons of 200 or more hits is the National League record for this century. In all of baseball, only Bill Terry hit for a higher average in those five seasons (.361). But Terry couldn't come close to Klein's power-hitting. The only season Chuck didn't lead the National League in homers, he instead set the all-time National League record with 107 extra-base hits and was second in home runs.

	HITS	B.A.	2B/3B/HR	RUNS	RBI
1929	219	.356	45/ 6/43*	126	145
1930	250	.386	*59/ 8/40	158*	170
1931	200	.337	34/10/31*	121*	121*
1932	226*	.348	50/15/38*	152*	137
1933	223*	.368*	*44/ 7/28*	101	120*
Average	224	.359	46/ 9/36	132	139
			(*Led NL)		

The young Klein came out of spring training as a Triple Crown threat every year, and finally pulled off the hat trick in 1933. But Chuck was more than just a hitter. He was a good defensive outfielder with a powerful, accurate arm. Three times in those five years he led the league in outfield assists including the all-time season record of 44 in 1930. Klein also had excellent speed and led the National League in stolen bases in 1932.

At age twenty-eight it looked as if Klein would collect well over 3,000 hits in his career, hit over 550 homers, set the all-time record for extra-base hits, and retire with the league record for runs scored and RBIs. Yet after his five awesome seasons

Klein never again led the league in any positive category.

Some suggest his career went downhill because he was traded away from the Phillies and their home park, Baker Bowl, which heavily favored left-handed hitters. Yet when Klein was traded back to the Phillies at age thirty-one, he still remained just a shadow of his former brilliant self.

What really happened to Chuck Klein can be traced to the 1933 season. Financial troubles had forced the Phillies to trade Chuck to Chicago in 1933. The Cubs paid a stiff price giving up three players as well as paying $65,000, a phenomenal sum during the Depression. Klein felt intense pressure to produce for Chicago, and teammate Billy Herman claims that Klein ended up destroying himself physically by trying to play through a severe leg injury.

"Klein got off to a great start with us after we got him from the Phillies, but then he pulled a hamstring muscle. He was a hell of a competitor, but he was just tearing up that leg. The blood started to clot in it, and I swear, that leg turned black, from his thigh all the way down to his ankle. I think it just about ruined his career. He couldn't run anymore; he couldn't swing the bat anymore."

The twenty-nine-year-old Klein—who had never hit below .337 before—averaged only .278 for the rest of his career. His ability to hit for power declined nearly 50 percent, and after hitting .218 at age thirty-five he was forced to retire to the coaching lines, a sad finish to what had been baseball's most brilliant beginning.

Chuck Klein (left) with Bill Terry.

Three Straight Errors
on Three Consecutive Balls

f you were asked to imagine the most horrible fielding performance in major-league history, how bad could it be? Could you make it the ninth inning, bases loaded, a three-run lead, and then have one player boot three straight batted balls to allow four runs to score and lose the game? Nah, too unrealistic—or is it?

Tommy "The Rabbit" Glaviano came up to the Cardinals as a nimble infielder with a reputation for being slightly error prone. In 1950, his first full season, he was placed at third base and got off to a fine start both at bat and in the field, where he showed tremendous range.

But on May 18, Glaviano put on the most embarrassing, disheartening fielding performance in the history of the game. His Cardinals had an 8-5 lead at Ebbets Field when the Dodgers loaded the bases in the ninth inning.

A grounder was then hit to Glaviano, who fielded it and threw wide of second as one run scored, and the bases remained loaded. The next batter hit another grounder to Glaviano, who threw wild again to allow another score and keep the bases loaded.

Pee Wee Reese then hit a third grounder to Glaviano. He had a chance to put the whole evil day behind him: he could throw home to force out the tying run, maybe even start a double play to set up a final out and seal the victory. But Glaviano never even got a chance for a third wild throw. The grounder skipped between his legs for an error that scored the tying and winning runs.

In the ninth inning, Glaviano had erred on *three consecutive ground balls*, each with the bases loaded, to turn an 8-5 lead into a 9-8 loss.

The game was not the only loss that resulted from this fielding disaster; there was also the matter of Glaviano's career. He did end up with the lowest fielding percentage among starting third basemen, but overlooked was his fine range at the position. The Rabbit also fielded far more balls *cleanly* per game than any other third baseman in the league. Still, Glaviano was ribbed mercilessly for his fielding disaster in Brooklyn, and the Cardinals destroyed what little confidence he had left by replacing him at third and trying to convert him to the outfield.

At the plate, Glaviano's rookie season was a clear success. He hit .285 and had an on-base percentage of .414 as the Cardinal's leadoff man. He scored 92 runs while playing just 115 games. But Glaviano was replaced by veteran Billy Johnson, who was acquired from the Yankees. Johnson hit a mediocre .266 but he did lead the league in fielding percentages at third base—without Glaviano's fielding range.

As for The Rabbit, he played off the bench for three years and hit just .213 before being released at age twenty-nine. His once-promising career was the victim of one truly disastrous inning in the field.

Hack Wilson's Lost Homer

ack Wilson was an odd figure in baseball history. He stood only five-feet-six but packed 190 pounds on a barrel frame which seemed to feature all chest and no neck. His shirt collar was size 18, but his feet were so small that he wore a size 5½ shoe.

Wilson was a very heavy drinker who made the Hall of Fame on his spectacular early seasons before he drank away his reflexes. Although he retired with a .307 career average he had his last .300 year at age thirty. He played his last season at age thirty-four, hitting only .245 with six homers.

But through age thirty, he was one of the Chicago Cubs' greatest stars ever. Despite his physique, Wilson was surprisingly fast and played primarily in center field. Historically, he has been much maligned as a poor defensive player due to a couple of rough plays in the spotlight of the 1929 World Series. But he was good enough to lead all National League outfielders in balls caught in 1927.

Wilson's power was never a question. He was a two-time minor-league home run champion. He won one of his minor-league crowns despite missing a large chunk of the season, but he managed to tag thirty homers in just 322 at bats. When he joined the Cubs, Hack took four major-league home run crowns in his first five seasons. He also hit over .312 each year, including .356 in 1930.

Hack
Wilson

98

That season, 1930, secured Wilson's place in baseball history. Wilson astounded the baseball world by officially driving in 190 runs, the all-time major-league record. Recent research indicates that total is in error—Wilson actually drove in 191 runs that year.

The same year, Wilson hit 56 homers which is still the National League record. In a development separate from the RBI controversy, former Reds catcher Clyde Sukeforth admits Wilson's record should really be 57 homers. In 1930 Sukeforth was sitting in the Cincinnati bullpen when Wilson hit one into the seats so hard that it bounced back onto the field; the umpire, however, ruled it had come off the screen on top of the wall. The whole Cincinnati bullpen saw what had actually happened, but they understandably told the umpire he'd made a helluva good call.

Any way you score it, Hack Wilson was one of the greatest sluggers in the game.

Cannon Ball Bill Stemmyer,
Entrenched in the Record Book

ill Stemmyer was a tall, stocky kid out of Cleveland, Ohio, signed by the Boston Red Stockings late in 1885. The twenty-year-old right-hander made an immediate impression by throwing a shutout in his first major-league start. The next season he became Boston's number-two pitcher based on a tremendous fastball, which earned him the nickname of Cannon Ball Bill.

They could just as easily have called him "Wild Bill" because of his horrible control. In that first full season, he led the league in strikeouts per inning, but he also led in walks per inning. He averaged close to four walks per nine innings which is poor even by modern standards. It really stood out in 1886, when the number of balls for a walk was raised from *six* to *seven*. Stemmyer managed to issue 144 of these seven-ball walks, giving him a walk rate almost double the rest of the Boston staff.

Yet Cannon Ball Bill still turned in the best ERA on the staff and was Boston's only pitcher with a winning record. Unfortunately, Stemmyer came up with a bad arm the very next season and made only sixteen more starts in his career before being forced to retire at age twenty-three.

Yet in that 1886 season Bill was able to grab a bit of immortality that is sure to keep him in the record book. Now what kind of record would you expect from a pitcher like Cannon Ball Bill Stemmyer, featuring all speed and no control?

Well, Mr. Cannon Ball threw so hard that his pitches were difficult to block and hold with the inferior gloves of the nineteenth-century catchers. In 1886, Stemmyer tossed an astounding *sixty-four* wild pitches. Most teams don't throw that many wild pitches in a full season!

Sixty-four wild pitches is more than twice the modern National League record of thirty. It's better than 2½ times the American League record of twenty-four set by Jack Morris in 1987. Cannon Ball Bill's record has stood for over a hundred years and seems safe for another century—or two—or three.

Wes Ferrell,
Baseball's Best-Hitting Pitcher

nly arm trouble at age thirty kept Wes Ferrell from being a Hall of Fame pitcher. He is the only hurler in this century to win twenty games in each of his first four full seasons. He ended up with six twenty-win seasons and 193 career wins despite winning only three games after age thirty.

Amazingly, a lot of people thought Wes could have made the Hall of Fame as an outfielder. As it is, he is generally recognized as baseball's greatest hitting pitcher. He holds the record for career homers by a pitcher (38) as well as the single-season record for homers (9) and RBIs (32) at the position. His career slugging percentage of .451 as a pitcher is also an all-time record.

Wes Ferrell

It was fairly typical that when Ferrell threw the only no-hitter of his career, he also doubled and homered for four RBIs. After his arm trouble ended his major-league career, Wes went on to become a player-manager in the minors where he was often his own best hitter. In 1942, he led the Virginia League in hitting with a .361 average, and also led in homers with 31.

Among his talented brothers, Wes was always considered the best hitter. One brother, George Ferrell, was a minor-league star for twenty years, hitting .321 with good power. His brother Rick Ferrell played eighteen years in the majors as a catcher and eventually made it to the Hall of Fame.

It is in comparison to his brother Rick that Wes Ferrell's bat is truly appreciated. You can break their records down in a number of ways, but it is Wes Ferrell, the pitcher, who always outhit Rick Ferrell, the Hall of Fame catcher. As a pinch hitter, Wes hit 72 points higher than Rick. When they were in the lineup, Wes hit .287 to Rick's .282.

Despite hitting ninth most of his career, Wes averaged 80 runs scored and 96 RBIs for every 600 plate appearances, a ratio that most outfielders would be proud of. By comparison, catcher Rick averaged only 59 runs scored and 63 RBIs.

The biggest difference between the two was in their power. Rick, as an everyday player, had over five times as many career at bats as his pitcher-brother, yet Wes hit ten more homers than Rick. Wes' home run ratio was actually *seven times* greater than that of his Hall of Fame brother.

Wes Ferrell would not have been another Babe Ruth as an outfielder, but he was the Babe Ruth of pitchers.

Dickey Pearce, Baseball Pioneer

lthough Dickey Pearce played only thirty-three major-league games, his impact can be found in every baseball game played in the last hundred years. He was born in 1836, and despite growing to a height of only five-feet-three, the Brooklyn native was recognized as one of the best fielders and smartest players in the New York area.

Pearce was an average hitter, but one day he got the idea of just holding the bat in the path of the pitch and letting the ball drop on the infield. Being a rather fast runner, Pearce often beat the play out for a hit. Yes, folks, Dickey Pearce had invented the bunt. It was especially effective in his day when the rules stated that a fair ball only had to hit once in fair territory. Pearce occasionally collected a double on a bunt that he laid down with such English that it skittered sideways into the crowd.

But Pearce's real moment of inventive genius occurred in the field. In the early days of baseball, only the basemen and the pitcher played on the infield. The shortstop was actually a fourth outfielder similar to a softball "rover" whose job is to catch the flares and short flies to the outfield.

In 1856, the twenty-year-old Pearce decided there were more grounders going through for hits between second and third base than there were flyballs that he was able to reach. Dickey had a strong throwing arm and decided to position himself on the outer edge of the infield between second and third base. From there he could still go back and catch an occasional flyball, but he could also snare a few of those groundballs and, with his strong arm, throw the batter out at first.

Technically, Pearce's throws to first were outfield assists, but soon everyone was moving their shortstops in toward the diamond, and the shortstop became classified as an infielder. In starting the conversion of the shortstop position, Pearce had set off the most significant defensive strategy change in the history of baseball.

Pearce went on to become a star player before the advent of professional leagues. Although he was thirty-five years old and past his prime when the first professional league formed in 1871, Pearce was a charter member of the New York Mutuals and a regular player throughout the league's five-year existence.

When baseball's first major league formed in 1876, the forty-year-old shortstop became a utility player for the St. Louis Reds in the National League. It was only fitting that Dickey Pearce, father of the bunt and the shortstop position, lasted long enough to earn a listing in *The Baseball Encyclopedia.*

The Toughest Pitcher to Beat in Major-League History

Surgeon Ferdinand Chandler did not look like the kind of pitcher who would set any significant records. The son of a good Georgia family, his college education came first. He did not turn professional until he was nearly twenty-five years old, and it took him another four-and-a-half seasons to get to the majors. Finally, in 1937, Spud made it to the pitching-rich Yankees as a twenty-nine-year-old rookie.

Chandler's struggles were hardly over. He was only a marginal performer, and a sore arm briefly sent him back to the minors. By age thirty-two he had won only 32 major-league games and was close to vanishing from the majors for good.

Spud's career began to take off in 1941 when he began to rely heavily on a nickel curve—what we now call a slider. Suddenly Chandler seemed unbeatable. From age thirty-three on, his winning percentage was an incredible .740; his ERA was 2.33.

In 1943 he won twenty games and lost only four while leading the league with a 1.64 ERA. Although Chandler was thirty-six years old, he enlisted in World War II the next season and served two years till the end of the war.

When the major leagues were back at full strength in 1946, Chandler continued to dominate in spite of his age. He was the Yankees' best pitcher, winning 20 games against only 8 defeats. His 2.10 ERA was second in the league. The next season was his last, but he still managed to go 9-5 and throw enough innings to qualify for the ERA title, which he won with a 2.46 mark.

How good was Spud Chandler? Because he was such a late bloomer and had his best year in 1943, a war year, historians frequently overlook him as one of the top pitchers in the 1940s. But the assessment of his peers is universally impressive. Ted Williams ranked him among the three toughest pitchers to hit. Hall of Famer Joe

Spud Chandler

McCarthy managed twenty-four years, including some of the greatest teams in the history of the Cubs, Yankees, and Red Sox, and he called Chandler one of the three finest pitchers he ever managed. McCarthy claimed that Chandler had a special feel for what it took to win games, and the record bears him out.

Even when he was a young and struggling pitcher, Chandler never had a losing season. Despite the shortness of his career, he helped *seven* Yankee teams win the pennant. In World Series competition he had a sparkling 1.62 ERA. But the greatest testimony to Spud Chandler's ability is that among pitchers with at least one hundred career victories, the highest winning percentage doesn't belong to Cy Young or Walter Johnson or Lefty Grove or Sandy Koufax—but to Spud Chandler with a mark of .717.

The Home Run
King before the Babe

ome fans still feel uncomfortable that Roger Maris, a talented but clearly lesser player, broke Babe Ruth's single-season home run record. What they need to hear is the story of Ned Williamson, the man who held the single-season home run record *before* Babe Ruth.

Ned Williamson was a pretty good all-around player from the nineteenth century who lasted thirteen seasons in the majors from 1878 to 1890. Williamson played for the Chicago entry in the National League. Rather than the Cubs, they were known as the Colts and sometimes as the White Stockings. They were the top team of the 1880s and Ned Williamson was one of their star players, but better known for his defensive prowess at third base than for his hitting skill. He hit only .255 in his career, but he played on six pennant winners, including his record-breaking season in 1884 when he stunned the baseball world by jumping the single-season home run record from 14 to 27.

What made his home-run performance so startling was that even though Ned was a star player, one thing he was not was a power hitter. Prior to his 27-homer outburst he had never hit more than three in a season and he never topped eight homers after his record season. Take out 1884 and in his other twelve seasons combined he hit only 36 homers.

What happened in 1884? The answer can be found in their ballpark and a change in the ground rules. In 1883, the Colts rebuilt their ballpark with bleachers in the outfield. That considerably cut down the outfield area to the smallest in major-league history. The right-field foul line went out only 196 feet and the power alley in right center was only 252 feet from home plate.

The first season, any ball hit over the right-field fence was automatically a ground-rule double. Then in 1884 they closed off the right-field bleachers and built a 20-foot wooden fence with a 17-foot tarpaulin on top. Any ball hit over that 37-foot wall in 1884 was a home run.

The new wall didn't work very well. It's easy enough to see what happened to Ned Williamson and the Colts in 1884:

	2B	3B	HR
1883 Colts	277*	61	13
1884 Colts	162	50	142*
1883 Williamson	49*	5	2
1884 Williamson	18	8	27*
	(*led league)		

What had been 1883 ground-rule doubles turned into 1884 home runs. For the record, of Ned Williamson's 27 home runs, 25 were hit in his home games—giving new meaning to the word "home" run.

The next year Williamson and the Colts moved into the Congress Street Grounds,

104

which had foul lines of only 216 feet, but the outfield fence had a bathtub shape that quickly deepened in the power alleys. Chicago's home runs fell from 142 to 55, and Williamson's home-run total dove from 27 to 3.

In 1919 Babe Ruth broke Ned's record by belting 29 homers. The next season he literally doubled Williamson's record with 54 homers. Still, Ned would have the last laugh. Babe's record of 60 homers in 1927 lasted thirty-four years until broken by Roger Maris in 1961. Williamson's home-run record lasted thirty-five years, one year longer than the Babe's.

The 1906 White Sox
Upset Baseball's All-Time Winners

The 1906 Chicago White Sox were destiny's children. Even when things went wrong they tended to come out right.

For example, their weak-hitting third baseman, Lee Tannehill, took his most valuable swing of the season during a warm-up when he accidentally swung into the face of a second baseman Gus Dondun. Poor Gus suffered a broken jaw and lost half his teeth, but the team also lost his bat, which had produced only a .192 average the year before. Gus' injury opened the door for Frank Isbell, who filled the position well in the field, led the team with a .279 average during the regular season, and hit .308 in the World Series.

The 1906 Chicago World Series.

In that Series, the White Sox had to face the most successful team in baseball history, the Chicago Cubs, winners of a record 116 games. Yet even this came out to the White Stockings' advantage. The Cubs had the key pitcher of the series in Mordecai "Three-Finger" Brown, who had a record setting 1.04 ERA. But because both teams were in Chicago, there were no travel dates in the Series and Brown would have to pitch on short rest if they wanted him to start three games.

The Sox suffered another injury just before the World Series and, again, it turned out to be a blessing in disguise. On the first day of the Series, White Sox shortstop and cleanup hitter George Davis hurt his back and was unable to play, which put utility player George Rohe in the lineup. Rohe hit so well that when Davis was able to return, Rohe moved to third base and played the rest of the Series. In fact, Rohe could easily be seen as the MVP of the Series. He played every game and led both teams with a .333 average and .571 slugging percentage.

And yes, the Series was decided when the Cubs tried to sneak in a third start for their star pitcher Three-Finger Brown, who had beaten the White Sox 1-0 in game 4. But this time Brown was working on just one day's rest. The Sox trounced Brown for seven runs, knocking him out of the game in the second inning. After their ace was out of the game, the Cubs went on to outscore the Sox 3-1, but the damage was already done and the White Sox were World Champions in one of the greatest upsets in World Series history.

Casey Stengel, World Series Hero

asey Stengel took part in ten World Series as a manager of the Yankees, but few fans know that Casey was also a talented player and a World Series hero.

Young Charlie Stengel picked up his nickname of "Casey" from the initials of his hometown, Kansas City. He was a left-handed-hitting outfielder whose career spanned fourteen seasons from 1912 to 1925.

Casey appeared in his first World Series in 1916 with the Brooklyn Dodgers and hit an impressive .368. He was later traded to John McGraw's New York Giants where he was used very effectively as a platoon player. In his two full seasons with New York he hit .355, and the club won the pennant both years.

The first year Casey got only five at bats in the World Series, but he had two hits for a .400 average. In the 1923 Series he played in all six games and had an even better Series, with a nifty .417 average. Playing in three World Series, Casey never hit less than .368 and overall averaged just under .400 (.393).

But Stengel is remembered more for his clutch World Series homers than for his high averages. Ironically, Stengel's World Series heroics with the Giants took place at the expense of the New York Yankees, the club that would eventually be so firmly linked with his Hall of Fame credentials as a manager. In the first game of the 1923 World Series, the Giants and Yankees were all tied up 4-4 going into the ninth.

Stengel belted a ball into the center-field gap in spacious Yankee Stadium and came around on a dramatic inside-the-park home run to win the game.

Then, in the seventh inning of the third game of the Series, Stengel belted a ball into the right-field seats to win the game 1-0. It was the first time in World Series history that a 1-0 game was won on a home run.

Those also happened to be the only two games that the Giants won in that Series. Naturally Stengel was stunned when the Giants traded him to the Boston Braves in the off-season. Casey told reporters: "I don't understand it. After two straight seasons over .330, I just hit .417 in the World Series with two game-winning homers. I guess I should count myself lucky that I didn't hit a third homer; they might have sent me to Topeka."

The New York Giants' Hall of Fame Infield

When shortstop Travis Jackson was elected to the Hall of Fame in 1982, it meant that the New York Giants had played with an infield of Hall of Famers for a record three seasons beginning in 1925. What makes the feat even more unusual is that they used a different second baseman each year, and in two of the seasons they actually had five Hall of Fame infielders.

In 1925 they had Memphis Bill Terry at first base, High Pockets Kelly at second, Travis "Stonewall" Jackson at shortstop, and Freddie Lindstrom at third base. They also had a very active utility infielder who played 120 games divided among

High Pockets Kelly, Frankie Frisch, Travis Jackson, and Heinie Groh of the New York Giants.

second, third, and short. His name was Frankie Frisch, and he ended up a better player than any of the starting four.

In 1926, Kelly was moved to first to make room for Frisch at second base. That made Bill Terry the odd man out, and the twenty-seven-year-old Hall of Famer got only 225 at bats as a part-time first baseman and the club's leading pinch-hitter.

In 1927, the Giants shook up their Hall of Fame infield by trading George Kelly to Cincinnati for Hall of Fame outfielder Ed Roush. Then they peddled Frankie Frisch to St. Louis for their new second baseman, Hall of Famer Rogers Hornsby.

Their infield streak of Hall of Famers came to an end in 1928 when Hornsby was shipped to the Boston Braves and the less-than-immortal Andy Cohen took over at second base.

Several students of the game have openly questioned the Hall of Fame qualifications of half these Giant infielders. No one disagrees that Frankie Frisch and Rogers Hornsby are deserving Hall of Famers, and Bill Terry's election was pretty much expected, but George Kelly, Freddie Lindstrom, and Travis Jackson remain three of the weakest selections ever made by the Hall.

Ironically, the Giants won the pennant in 1924, the year before their first Hall of Fame infield. Yet they finished second, fifth, and third after assembling their famous infield.

In 1928, the first year after the infield was broken up, the Giants finished a very strong second, winning ninety-three games. That's better than any of the three years when they had Hall of the Fame infields. In fact, the Giants had a losing record in 1926 and averaged only eighty-four wins for the three seasons with their infield—hardly what you'd expect from such a stellar assemblage.

The Missing Seasons of Ted Williams

Ted Williams managed to put up some impressive career totals including 521 home runs and 1,839 RBIs, which ranks tenth in all of baseball history, and the famed left fielder of Fenway did all this despite being the only major-league player to lose five years of his career to military service.

When World War II interrupted Ted's career for three years, he was at his absolute prime as a ballplayer. In each of the two years prior to his service, he led the league in both batting average and home runs. In 1941 he had his famous .400-season, and in 1942 he took the Triple Crown.

Ted was twenty-seven when he returned to the Red Sox in 1946 and promptly won the league's Most Valuable Player award. The next year he became the only player in the history of the American League to twice take the Triple Crown.

During the war, Williams had opted for aviation and become a Marine pilot. Because of his special skill, Williams was called back to active duty in the Korean War at age thirty-four to serve nearly two full years (1952-53). Ted was still an impressive player at the time and led the league in slugging percentage the year before and the year after his Korean service.

Williams lost nearly 700 games and well over 2,000 at bats while serving his country. An attempt to replace those five missing seasons with reasonable estimates based on his performance levels before and after each service hitch gives an impressive facelift to what is an already awesome record:

Estimate of Williams' Career without Military Service									
AB	H	B.A.	2B	3B	HR	Slug%	BBs	Runs	RBIs
10,057	3,481	.346	684	101	693	.641	2,712	2,395	2,425

Estimated Changes in Major League Records

Most RBIs, Williams passes Aaron by 218
Most Runs Scored, Williams passes Cobb by 150
Most Extra-Base Hits, Williams passes Aaron by 1
Most Walks, Williams passes Ruth by 656
Most Times Reaching Base (H + W), Williams passes Rose by 371
Most Years Leading League in RBIs, Williams ties Ruth at 6
Most Years Leading League in Slugging Percentage, Williams ties Ruth at 13
Most Years Leading League in Runs Scored, Williams' 9 to Ruth's 8
Most Years Leading League in Walks, Williams' 16 to Ruth's 11

This type of adjustment explains why so many of Ted's contemporaries stood in awe of his hitting ability and called him the greatest hitter in baseball history.

Jerry Denny,
the Last of the Barehanded Breed

When Jeremiah Eldridge decided to take up baseball as a career in 1880, his New York family disapproved, claiming that such a career was an embarrassment to the family name. So Jerry, whose middle name was Dennis, dropped his last name and became a player named Jerry Denny — a significant footnote in baseball history.

On the surface, Jerry's career record does not suggest anything noteworthy. He did manage to last thirteen seasons in the National League, an unusually long career in nineteenth-century baseball, but his career batting average was only .260. The only category in which he ever led the league was most strikeouts by a batter, in 1888.

The secret to Jerry's longevity was his fielding skill and versatility. He was best known as a third baseman, but he played every position at least once in his

Jerry
Denny

major-league career. Denny's fielding prowess was especially noteworthy because of his absolute refusal to wear the new fielding gloves which came into use at every position in the late 1880s. While the great nineteenth-century second baseman Bid McPhee is recognized as the last player to play major-league baseball barehanded, McPhee eventually gave in and started using a glove late in his career.

Jerry Denny was the last true disciple of barehanded play, the last major leaguer who never wore a glove in the field. Jerry had a very good reason for his bare-handed style. Although he was normally right-handed and batted as a right-hander, he was totally ambidextrous in the field.

Denny remained resistant to the newfangled gloves because they would have required his learning to backhand a ball, something he had never done. He had always fielded the ball with whichever hand was closest to the play.

Jerry took his ambidextrous fielding one step further. He usually threw right-handed because that was his stronger arm, but if he was pressed for time when he fielded a ball with his left hand, he would simply throw it left-handed. Denny's barehanded ambidextrous fielding paid off, as five times he led the league in chances fielded per game at third base. And it gave an otherwise obscure player a place in the baseball record books.

The 1943 Athletics
and the Infamous Balata Ball

n 1943, World War II was causing a serious rubber shortage, and the major leagues experimented with a a rubber substitute surrounding the core of the baseballs. The substance was known as Balata, the same material that covers most golf balls. The Balata ball looked perfectly normal but the new core cover significantly reduced the ball's resiliency. Some estimates were as high as 25 percent, suggesting that what should have been four-hundred-foot homers were going to be caught as three-hundred-foot fly balls.

By April 29, the entire American League had hit only two home runs. The fans hated baseball with the Balata ball and a quick decision was made to return to the old core. By May 9, no more Balata balls were shipped to the major leagues, although balls from the original shipment continued to surface from time to time throughout the season.

Overall, shutouts were up 13 percent while home runs declined 15 percent. The team affected the most by the Balata ball was the Philadelphia Athletics, who were horrible with or without the Balata ball. They not only lost 105 games to finish 49 games behind the pennant-winning Yankees, but they also finished a full 20 games behind the next-to-last-place team.

The Athletics set an American League record of twenty straight losses that lasted forty-six years until broken by the 1988 Baltimore Orioles. One record the 1943 Athletics aren't likely to surrender is their feat of losing *eighteen* doubleheaders! And even if you threw out those thirty-six losses, they still would have ended up in last place.

Part of their problem was an offense that looked as if it had a lifetime supply of Balata balls. Left fielder Bobby Estalella was the only man on the club who hit more than three homers. The whole team combined for just twenty-six homers, and they were also dead last in doubles with only 174. Their team slugging percentage ended up at .297, making them the only team in the history of the Live-Ball Era (since 1920) to slug under .300. Whether it was the Balata ball or just lousy hitting, for the Philadelphia Athletics, 1943 was a year to forget.

The Weak Bat of Tommy Thevenow

L ittle Tommy Thevenow played fifteen years in the majors as a shortstop and utility infielder, primarily with the Cardinals and Pirates.

He was an excellent fielder with tremendous range. He had only two seasons where he played more than 120 games in the field. Both times he led all shortstops in putouts and assists. In 1926 when he started for the World Champion Cardinals he had over a hundred more assists than any other shortstop. The next year Thevenow got off to a bad start, hitting only .194 and then missing the last hundred games with a broken leg. The Cardinals finished in second place, and manager Bob O'Farrell said the club would have repeated if they could have kept Thevenow's glove in the field.

Thevenow was never much of a hitter. He was five-feet-ten and a skinny 155 pounds. His hitting style was simply to slap the ball in play and try to beat the throw to first. His career batting average is only .233, and in fifteen seasons covering over 4,000 at bats he never hit a ball out of the park. Both of his career home runs were inside-the-park homers.

Tommy Thevenow

Not only couldn't Thevenow hit it out of the park, he had a hard time just getting it past the outfielders. He averaged fewer than twenty extra-base hits every 500 at bats, and his career slugging percentage is a measly .294.

Imagine the surprise of the fans when it was the bat of little Tommy Thevenow that sparked the Cardinals to victory over Babe Ruth's Yankees, four games to three, in the 1926 World Series. Barely a month past his twenty-third birthday, Tommy found himself outhitting stars like Ruth, Gehrig, and Hornsby in baseball's showcase series.

Thevenow's .417 average led all hitters, and in game 2 Tommy hit a ball into the left center field gap of Yankee Stadium and came around on an inside-the-park home run.

Thevenow's hitting performance was the shock of the Series, but no one expected that his home run would be the last of his career. Thevenow played twelve more years and never homered again. He ended up going 3,347 at bats without a home run of any kind, and *that* is a major-league record.

Yet, in a great bit of baseball irony, Thevenow still has more *World Series* homers than Hall of Famers like Ty Cobb, Ted Williams, and Ernie Banks.

The Schoolboy Shortstop

ost trivia buffs can tell you that Joe Nuxhall, at age fifteen, is the youngest "man" to ever play in the majors. But Nuxhall's claim is based on a single relief appearance of just two-thirds of an inning. He was bombed and never seen in the majors again until he was a man of twenty-four. The only legitimate schoolboy regular in major-league history is Tommy "Buckshot" Brown.

Tommy was a Brooklyn schoolboy who became the Dodgers' regular shortstop in August of 1944 after shortstop Bobby Bragen was drafted into the Army. Tommy was just sixteen years old, and in forty-six games he hit a lowly .164. Brown had pretty good range in the field and a strong arm, but the accuracy of his throws left a lot to be desired. Once he set himself for a throw to first base and launched the ball into the upper deck. His powerful but erratic throws earned him the nickname of "Buckshot."

Brown also became known for making one of the most unusual fielding errors in baseball history. One day Buckshot misread a ball which bounced cleanly between his legs. Tommy went through the motion of fielding the ball and then made a phantom throw to first base. He did such a convincing job of it that Dodger left fielder Augie Galan really thought Brown had fielded the ball. Augie was then surprised to see, out of the corner of his eye, a ball skipping to the outfield fence. By the time he had retrieved the ball, the batter had circled the bases. Tommy Brown ended up being charged with a unique four-base error.

But for all of his struggles, Buckshot Brown was back with the Dodgers in the summer of 1945. Brooklyn used concert violinist Eddie Bissinski at shortstop until Tommy could get out of school, and Buckshot did much better his second time around the league. He hit a respectable .245 and in August he connected for a home run off Preacher Roe of Pittsburgh. Brown was still only seventeen years old and remains the youngest player to ever hit a major-league home run.

After the war, Brown spent one year in the minors, but was back in the majors while still a teenager at age nineteen. He played seven more years as a bench player, with occasional signs of brilliance. In 1950 he hit three consecutive homers for the Dodgers, and in 1952 he hit .320 in sixty-one games with the Cubs. But in between were a lot of weak .240 seasons and he finally retired from professional baseball at the ripe old age of twenty-five.

The Louisville Slugger

Pete "The Gladiator'" Browning was a hitting star from the nineteenth century. He played thirteen years in the major leagues from 1882 to 1894. Pete won three batting titles and five other times finished among the top three in batting average. He retired with a lifetime batting average of .343 which is the tenth-highest in major-league history.

Yet Browning is not in baseball's Hall of Fame, and he probably doesn't deserve the honor because of his serious shortcomings as a fielder. Most of Pete's troubles in the field can be traced to his extreme bouts with mastoiditis, which destroyed his middle ear and caused him to go partially deaf. He started as an infielder, but he kept getting blind-sided by runners he didn't hear coming and collided with other infielders he couldn't hear calling for the ball. He switched to the outfield, but the damage to his middle ear gave him a poor sense of balance and made it difficult for him to accurately judge flyballs. It's a wonder he was able to hit as well as he did. In 1887, he hit for the highest average of his career, .402, but he also led the league's outfielders with forty-six errors, fifteen more than anyone else.

Browning drank heavily to relieve the pain of his illness and tragically, became an alcoholic. By age thirty-two he could no longer play regularly. He played only three more games at age thirty-three and retired. He eventually died young at age forty-four.

Pete never got to the Hall of Fame, but he did leave a legacy which can be found in bat racks all over the country. Pete was a native of Louisville, Kentucky, and played most of his major-league career in that city, first in the American Association and then in the National League. On July 15, 1887, a young man named John "Bud" Hillerich was in the stands when Browning broke his bat.

Young Hillerich offered to make Pete a new bat at his father's woodworking shop. Bud took a piece of sturdy white ash and lathed it to Browning's specifications. Thus was born the first Louisville Slugger—a bat made for Pete Browning.

When Pete went 3 for 3 with his new bat, his teammates started asking young Bud to customize their bats. Hillerich eventually went into the bat-making business full-time and registered the Louisville Slugger trademark in 1894. Ironically, 1894 was also the last major-league season for Pete "The Gladiator" Browning, the original Louisville Slugger.

Pete "The Gladiator" Browning in 1888.

The Day the Fans
Managed the St. Louis Browns

Bill Veeck will always be remembered as the man who sent a midget to the plate, but his most daring promotion was the day he let the fans manage his 1951 St. Louis Browns.

The first step was to find the right opponent and quiet the charges that Veeck would be making a mockery of the game. The natural choice was Connie Mack's Philadelphia Athletics. Their club was as hopelessly out of the race as were the Browns. And despite what one would expect from the Hall of Fame manager with the starched collars, Mr. Mack always enjoyed Veeck's wild promotions, and Bill often tried to schedule something special when the Athletics came to town. This one would end up as Connie Mack's all-time favorite.

With the date set, the Browns' fans were given ballots weeks ahead of time to vote for their starting lineup. The fans who voted were entitled to sit behind first base where they were given large cards saying "YES" on one side and "NO" on the other.

St. Louis Browns fans voting on a strategy question.

During the game, a coach standing on the dugout would hold up a sign with a strategy question—like whether to bunt or hit-and-run, to warm-up a pitcher, or pull the starter. A quick estimate of the YES's and NO's determined the strategy which was relayed by walkie-talkie to the dugout.

How did this democracy in action turn out? Well, the fans made two changes in the normal lineup. They put Sherm Lollar behind the plate and Hank Arft at first base. This proved to be a spark of genius as these two players ended up driving in all of the Browns' runs.

Lollar had three hits, scored three runs, and hit a three-run homer. Arft knocked in two more to give the Browns a 5-3 victory. The fans retired with a 1.000 winning percentage and are still waiting for a courageous club to hire them again.

And what about the Browns' regular manager? Well, Zack Taylor watched the game from a rocking chair while smoking a pipe and wearing slippers in place of his spikes. Maybe Old Zack should have paid closer attention. When he took over the club again, they promptly lost five of their next six games. Taylor was fired at the end of the season and retired with the lowest winning percentage of any manager with over 600 decisions.

The All-Time Iron Glove Performance

ammy Davis was the regular second baseman for Baton Rouge in the Evangeline League in 1952. Although Davis was technically playing Class C ball, he was there mostly for his bat as his fielding was pure Class F. Davis led the team with 105 runs scored in his 122 games, but he also led the league's second basemen with forty-five errors in just 111 games.

Oddly enough, Baton Rouge was known for its well-kept diamond, and their official scorers were not known for their harshness. Baton Rouge's regular first baseman and shortstop led their positions in fielding percentage. And when short-stop Bill Vega filled in for seventeen games at second base, he made only one error in 106 chances, an excellent fielding percentage of .991 compared to Davis' dismal .934.

As bad as Davis was, he would be forgotten today if it weren't for an injury to Vega early in the year. Davis was shifted over as a replacement shortstop for a few games, but he was quickly replaced by third baseman Luther Payer. Luther played thirty-two games at short and didn't do very well as his poor fielding percentage of .873 clearly indicates. Yet he was a dramatic improvement over Sammy Davis who had made twenty-one errors in his eleven games at shortstop—nearly two a game for a fielding percentage of .731.

Sammy Davis was playing shortstop when he made baseball history on May 7, 1952. In this century the major-league record for errors in a game by a single player is six. That happened way back in 1904 when shortstop Bill O'Neill made six miscues in an extra-inning game that went thirteen innings. Playing against New

Iberia, Baton Rouge shortstop Sammy Davis set the all-time record for professional baseball by erring *eight* times in an eleven-inning game.

Appropriately enough, Davis' fielding—or lack of fielding—managed to end the nightmare game. His eighth error, a low throw to first, allowed in the winning run that beat Baton Rouge 4-3.

Jim Tobin, the Home-Run-Hitting Pitcher

Jim Tobin was one of many knuckleball pitchers who were active in the 1940s. He lasted nine seasons, playing mostly with the Pirates and Braves, and his pitching highlights were few and far between.

In 1942, he was the hardest-working pitcher in the National League, leading in both innings pitched and complete games. In 1944, Tobin had his best season on the mound, winning a career-high eighteen games, but his Boston Braves were not much of a team, and he lost nineteen despite a 3.01 ERA. The next year, he was traded in mid-season to the pennant-bound Detroit Tigers and, as fate would have it, his last appearance in a big-league uniform came in the 1945 World Series.

Tobin's best game on the mound was in April of 1944. He threw a no-hitter against the Brooklyn Dodgers, and it was the first no-hitter by a Boston Braves pitcher in twenty-eight years. In the eighth inning Tobin gave the game his special trademark, a booming home run to left field.

Tobin was known as an excellent hitter. In his rookie season he had gone 15 for 34 for a nice little batting average of .441. But what folks remember about Tobin's hitting is his power. In 1942 he hit five homers to tie the National League record for home runs by a pitcher. He also became the only pitcher in this century to hit three homers in a single game. The truth is, he almost had four homers and nearly had a streak of five straight.

On May 12, Tobin had hit the only pinch-hit homer of his career. The next day he was the starting pitcher against the Cubs, and in his first at bat his long fly backed left fielder Swish Nicholson to the base of the wall. On Tobin's next three times up, all Nicholson could do was watch the ball sail into the seats. Tobin needed every bit of his own hitting support as he won the game by a margin of only one run, 6-5. But if Tobin had been able to add a few feet to his first blow, he would have hit four homers for the day to homer in five consecutive at bats.

Despite Tobin's home-run heroics in 1942, baseball trivia buffs remember his 1945 season best. Who is the only player to lead his position in home runs in both leagues —in the same year? Yes, it actually happened, and Jim Tobin is the man. In 1945, Tobin appeared in twenty-seven games while pitching for the Boston Braves and hit three home runs. He was then traded to the Detroit Tigers where he got into fourteen games as a pitcher and hit two more home runs. Both totals remain the league-leading figure for pitchers.

The Babe's Nemesis

T here is a popular baseball reference book with a category of "Hates to face:" that they run for each active player. If such a book were done on Hall of Famers, Babe Ruth's entry would say "Hates to face: Hub Pruett."

Yes, if any pitcher had the Babe's number, it was the obscure left-handed reliever Hub Pruett. The first time they met was on April 22, 1922.

Hub was a twenty-one-year-old rookie left-hander with the St. Louis Browns; the mighty Babe, at age twenty-seven, was in his physical prime. In the last two seasons he had hit .377 with consecutive seasons of 54 and 59 homers. Yet Pruett struck the Babe out on three pitches!

Pruett was that rarity—a left-handed pitcher who threw a screwball. Even though the left-handed scroogie would break in like a right-hander's curveball, for some

Hub Pruett

119

reason the pitch was almost impossible for the Babe to hit. The first five times Ruth faced Pruett, he struck out. Babe finally broke the strikeout string with a weak tapper back to the mound, but then he struck out five more times against Pruett.

Once during that streak the Browns found themselves facing Ruth with the bases loaded, and even though Pruett was in the starting rotation at that time, they brought Hub into the game simply to face the Babe. Pruett struck him out. The crowds loved this victory of the underdog, heightened by the fact that, next to the massive bulk of the Babe, Pruett, at five-feet-ten and 160 pounds, appeared to be David taking on Goliath.

Hub was very modest about striking out the game's greatest hitter ten times in eleven at bats. He told the press, "Shucks, I was just lucky against the Babe." When his teammates heard that, Pruett had a nickname which would stay with him his whole career, "Shucks" Pruett.

Babe eventually did get a hit and even a homer against Pruett in 1922, but Hub kept the edge in their future meetings. Babe retired with a .190 batting average and strikeouts in 50 percent of his thirty appearances against Pruett. The little lefty finished his rookie season with a fine 2.33 ERA, but after pitching in six straight games late in the year, his arm came up lame. He never again was an effective pitcher, but there were always teams willing to give a trial to the now-famous reliever.

"Shucks" Pruett managed to last six more seasons despite an ERA over 5.00 and a winning percentage under .350. Pruett knew the end of his career was just a matter of time and wisely saved his baseball earnings for a college education. The quiet little left-hander eventually became a physician and, remembering how he had earned the money that paid for his education, he often joked that Babe Ruth put him through medical school.

Babe Ruth —
The All-Around Athlete

 esides being the game's greatest power hitter, and before that one of the best left-handed pitchers, the Babe was known for his versatility and excellence in a number of sports. He was an avid golfer—not surprisingly, long off the tee—but he also possessed a remarkably delicate and accurate short game. In a 1935 tournament, he finished in the top 10 percent in a field of 226 of New York's best amateur golfers.

Babe also was quite comfortable and coordinated with either hand. Early in his career he was known to switch-hit on occasion against a tough lefty, and he was an excellent bowler from either side. In spring training he could beat nearly anyone in camp, bowling left- or right-handed. Ruth was an avid hunter known for his marksmanship and enjoyed ocean fishing as well.

In fact, the Babe seemed to have a knack for just about any sport he ever tried. Perhaps the best story of all comes from his tour of Europe after his retirement from baseball. Ruth was attending a party in England when he mentioned that he had broken nearly a thousand bats in his twenty-two year career. Ruth was informed that he should have used a cricket bat as they were known for their unusual durability. Cricket bats were flame-hardened, a treatment uncommon in baseball at the time.

A famous Australian cricketer named Alan Fairfax lured the Babe onto a cricket field and taught him the rudiments of a cricket swing. Babe struggled to make solid contact until he shifted to his baseball stance. On the Babe's next swing he blasted the ball farther than anyone had ever seen a cricket ball hit. On his second swing—he broke the bat.

Although Ruth was forty-two years old at the time, Fairfax said, "I wish I could have him for a fortnight. I'd make the world's greatest [cricket] batsman out of him."

Baseball's
Most Valuable Pinch Hitter

In the first fifty years of this century, when you talked about pinch-hitting you were sure to start with Charlie "Red" Lucas. The little five-foot-nine-inch, left-handed hitter played fifteen years in the majors from 1923 to 1938, mostly with the Cincinnati Reds and Pittsburgh Pirates. Four times he led the league in pinch-hits, including three consecutive years during which he had over 140 at bats as a pinch hitter and averaged .298

His best year in the pinch was 1930 when he hit .359 including a pinch-hit home run. When he retired, his career record of 114 pinch-hits stood for almost thirty years before being passed by Smokey Burgess. Since then, Lucas' 114 pinch-hits have slipped down to fifth place, and Lucas' career batting average as a pinch-hitter has also been surpassed by players like Burgess, Jose Morales, and Manny Mota.

On the surface, Burgess, Morales, and Mota were all better pinch-hitters than Lucas, but given a choice, just about any manager would prefer having Little Red as the key pinch hitter on his roster.

You see, the value of a pinch hitter is diminished by the cost to the team in terms of carrying him on the roster. Manny Mota collected better than half his career pinch-hits in seven seasons in which he totaled only sixteen appearances in the field. In those years the Dodgers were basically surrendering a roster spot just for the luxury of carrying Mota as a pinch hitter.

Red Lucas was never that kind of burden. For Lucas, pinch hitting was strictly a sideline to his real job with the club. You see, Lucas was a pitcher, and a darn good one. Red was one of the best control pitchers in baseball history. His average of 1.61 walks every nine innings is just behind Christy Mathewson's as the seventh-best walk rate in this century. Six times he led his team in wins. Three times he led the league in complete games. Pitching mostly with second division clubs, he won 157 games with an overall record of twenty-two games over .500.

Naturally, Red Lucas was also one of the best-hitting pitchers. When he wasn't

Charles "Red" Lucas

pinch hitting, he hit .289, the second-highest career average among pitchers with one thousand at bats in this century. After his retirement, Red continued to manage and coach in the minor leagues and served as his own best pinch hitter. In 1945, at age 43, Old Red managed to hit .423 as a pinch hitter for Nashville.

1954, the Year of the
Minor-League Walter Mittys

How rare is it for someone to suddenly step into a professional baseball game from outside the playing ranks *and* enjoy immediate success? Well, this Walter Mitty dream actually happened twice in the summer of 1954.

On April 24 of that year, Joe Carolan paid his way in to see a game between Columbus and Macon in the South Atlantic League. What made the day so unusual is that Joltin' Joe Carolan ended up making his professional debut in that very game.

Once in the park, the twenty-one-year-old talked his way into taking batting practice with the Columbus team. Carolan was a massive 230 pounds and socked several balls into the bleachers. He was immediately given a contract and told to suit up for the game. Joe started the game in the outfield, and in the true tradition of a Walter Mitty daydream, Joe hit a grand slam in his very first at bat!

Unfortunately, that was the extent of Joe's heroics. He appeared in only thirty-two more games, usually as a pinch hitter, and hit only .231. He quickly rejoined the other paying customers, but with a story good for a lifetime.

Later that same summer, another minor-league team went outside their player ranks to come up with an impressive performance. By September 5, 1954, the Asheville team in the Tri-State League had already clinched the pennant. That day they had a game with the second-place Knoxville team. The starting pitcher for Asheville was the groundskeeper for McCormick Field, their home park.

Charles "Bud" Shaney was a former minor-league pitcher, but had not pitched professionally in over a dozen years. Well, Old Bud, who was fifty-three years old at the time, pitched brilliantly. He was the winning pitcher in a 4-0 whitewash, allowing only 4 hits in his five innings.

When asked the secret of his success, Bud answered in good humor that the groundskeeper had done a heck of a job with the field, and the mound was just the way he liked it.

Baseball's
Most Underrated Pitcher

For some reason Ed Reulbach seems destined to be remembered less for his pitching feats than for his inability to impress the writers of his day and the baseball historians of the present.

Reulbach was one of the smarter ballplayers, coming to the Chicago Cubs from the University of Notre Dame, where he was an engineering student. He joined the Cubs in 1905 and immediately won eighteen games while turning in a 1.42 ERA, second-best in the league and third-best ever by a rookie pitcher in this century.

The next year he led the league in winning percentage with a 19-4 mark and posted the league's third-best ERA at 1.65. He capped off the season with a one-hit shutout in the 1906 World Series. He had a remarkably similar year the next season with a 1.69 ERA and a 17-4 record that again led the league in winning percentage. Again he starred in the World Series, allowing only six hits and one run in twelve innings of work. Yet researcher Bill James points out that the *Spalding Baseball Guide* of that season characterized Reulbach as "…effective at times but extremely wild and unreliable."

Well, "Unreliable" Reulbach went on to lead the league in winning percentage again in 1908, the first time a pitcher had ever led in that category for three consecutive seasons. The only other pitcher to match that mark has been Hall of Famer Lefty Grove.

Ed Reulbach

Reulbach has been ignored by the Hall of Fame despite some very impressive credentials. Because Reulbach made almost a hundred appearances as a relief pitcher, he fell eighteen wins short of 200 career victories, but he stacks up very well in two of the key categories. Among those with at least 175 career victories in this century, his .633 winning percentage ranks eighth. And his career ERA of 2.28 ranks seventh among those with 2,000 career innings. On both lists he is the only member of the top ten *not* in baseball's Hall of Fame.

Falling short of the Hall of Fame, Big Ed Reulbach should still be remembered for his awesome performance in the dramatic pennant race of 1908. His Cubs were involved in a tremendous battle with the Giants and Pirates that finally ended in the first playoff game in baseball history. The Cubs would never have made it through September without the strong right arm of Ed Reulbach.

The Cubs were facing a jammed-up schedule, due to a doubleheader with Brooklyn late in the month. The Dodgers had always struggled with Reulbach's outstanding curveball, and Big Ed had already beaten them seven times in seven attempts that year. On September 26, Reulbach pitched both ends of that double-header against Brooklyn. Big Ed not only won both games, but both wins were shutouts, a feat unmatched in baseball history.

Reulbach also pitched shutouts in his starts both before and after that double-header. In the fiercest pennant race in baseball history, Reulbach finished the season with a streak of forty-four consecutive shutout innings!

Baseball's
Least-Deserving Hall of Famer

Fans like to argue about whether certain borderline players deserve Hall of Fame recognition, but the Hall's least-deserving member is found among those inducted for meritorious service to the game as pioneers and executives. Few know who Morgan Bulkeley is, and no one can explain why he deserves such an honor.

When the National League was formed in 1876, Bulkeley was there simply as a representative of the Hartford club. The league needed a president and secretary, and rather than vote on the officers, the group decided to draw them from a hat. The first name drawn would be president and the second would be league secretary. To Bulkeley's chagrin, his name was the first drawn from the hat.

Bulkeley was a businessman with an interest in banking and politics. The business of baseball held little appeal for him, and he asked William Hulbert, who was basically the founder of the league, to take the presidency. But Hulbert declined and Morgan was stuck with the job. Bulkeley then agreed to take the job only if it were understood that his term would be limited to one year.

Bulkeley's one-year term was uneventful. The most controversial league meeting involved the decision to expel the New York Mutuals and Philadelphia Athletics for failing to complete their schedules, and Bulkeley didn't even show up for that meeting. Within a year, Bulkeley sold his interest in the Hartford club and was never officially associated with major-league baseball again. So how the heck did Morgan Bulkeley get into the Hall of Fame?

It turns out that in 1937, the Hall of Fame wanted to enshrine Ban Johnson, the first president of the American League, a true pioneer who was an influential figure in the game for over twenty-five years. To avoid offending the National League, the election committee decided to also put in the first league president for the senior circuit, who happened to be Morgan Bulkeley.

To be fair, Morgan Bulkeley was a significant *historical* figure in his era. He founded the United States Bank of Hartford and served as the town's mayor for nine years. He then served six years as the governor of Connecticut and another six years in the United States Senate. In 1896 he even received 39 votes for the Republican nomination for Vice President of the United States. But Bulkeley's place in baseball's Hall of Fame derived solely from the luck of his name being drawn from a hat in 1876.

Chick Hafey,
the Nearsighted Hall of Famer

Charles "Chick" Hafey was an outfielder who earned his fame with the St. Louis Cardinals in the 1920s and 1930s. The former pitcher was blessed with one of the strongest throwing arms of all time and had tremendous talent as a hitter.

Hafey played in four pennant winners and was a steady .300 hitter who finished with a career average of .317. Although he was basically a line-drive hitter, he still hit the ball hard enough to average forty doubles and twenty homers for every 150 games he played. In 1927, he edged out Rogers Hornsby and Hack Wilson to lead the National League in slugging percentage.

What made Hafey's success so phenomenal was that he had very poor eyesight that steadily deteriorated during his career. He also suffered from a severe sinus condition that required surgery four different times during his career, leaving him unusually susceptible to colds and flus. It was Hafey's health that forced him to retire at age thirty-two even though he was hitting .339 at the time.

Hafey attracts a lot of interest as the only Hall of Fame hitter who wore glasses, and they made a tremendous difference in his playing career. Chick was already nearsighted when he came to the big leagues, but he resisted wearing eyeglasses for his first five years in the majors. With his vision blurring more and more, he finally submitted to glasses in 1929.

Listening to the taunts of "Hey, Four Eyes!" proved to be worth it as Hafey immediately set career highs with a .338 batting average, twenty-nine homers, and 125 RBIs. Two years later, in 1931, he hit .349 and became the first man to win a batting championship while wearing glasses.

Even with his glasses, Hafey's eyesight was far from perfect. Teammates remember he still had trouble reading the large clocks in train depots, and his vision

Chick Hafey

became so bad that he had to be fitted with bifocals while still an active player.

Branch Rickey claimed, "If Hafey had had good eyesight and good health, he might have been the finest right-handed hitter baseball has every known." But he was still good enough for the Hall, and it won't be long before old "Four Eyes" Hafey is joined by another Hall of Famer who took to glasses in mid-career—Reggie Jackson.

The International Hall of Famer

hen the Hall of Fame finally opened its doors to the stars of the old Negro Leagues, it also paved the way for the first Cuban Hall of Famer, Martin Dihigo.

Young Martin first came to the United States in 1923 as a seventeen-year-old second baseman touring with a Cuban All-Star team. He later returned to the States to play in the Negro Leagues and quickly became a star outfielder. By age twenty-one he was hitting .331 and leading the league in home runs.

When he was 29, Dihigo led the league with a .372 average and managed his New York-based team to the pennant. Hall of Fame manager John McGraw saw him play several times and claimed Dihigo was the greatest natural player he had ever seen. At six-feet-three, 220 pounds, Dihigo was an awesome sight at the plate, and in the outfield he has been compared to Willie Mays with Roberto Clemente's arm.

In the 1930s, Dihigo's great throwing arm led him to take up pitching and he began a long pitching career in the newly formed Mexican League. He threw the first no-hitter in the history of the league and, in 1938, he went 18-2, led the league with a 0.90 ERA, and won the batting crown with a .387 batting average!

Probably the greatest single game in Dihigo's career came when he was still playing in the Negro Leagues. One year he found himself locked in a tight batting race that went right down to the final day of the season. Dihigo went into the last

Martin Dihigo

128

game tied for the league lead with teammate Willie Wells, the great black shortstop.

Wells hit third in the lineup and Dihigo was the cleanup hitter. As they entered the last inning, Wells was 3 for 3 with a walk and Dihigo was 4 for 4. In his last at bat, Wells singled to give him a perfect 4 for 4 day. Dihigo came to the plate knowing that his at bat would decide the batting title. Like a true legend, he made it a perfect 5 for 5 game by belting a home run and winning the batting championship.

Martin Dihigo was never allowed to play in the all-white major leagues, but he is the only player honored in the baseball Halls of Fame of Cuba, Mexico, and the United States—truly an international Hall of Famer.

Confusion Over a Coin Flip
Sets Up the Shot
Heard Round the World

n 1946, five years before Bobby Thomson squared off against Ralph Branca, the Dodgers had finished in a tie with the St. Louis Cardinals. Brooklyn won the coin flip to determine who would have the two home games in the best-of-three pennant playoff. Naturally, the Dodgers chose to have the home-field advantage. But they failed to take into account their thirteen-hour train ride to St. Louis to play the first game and their exhausting return trip the very next day.

The Dodgers lost that first game in St. Louis to the rested Cardinals. Then, after the Dodgers made the long return trip to Brooklyn, the exhausted players lost the second game and the pennant before they could enjoy their home-field advantage in the third game.

In 1951, when they flipped the coin for a possible playoff between the Dodgers and Giants, most of the Brooklyn front office were with the team on a road trip. Representing the Dodgers was ticket manager Jack Collins, who won the flip. With the Giants and Dodgers just across the river from each other, there was no danger of the 1946 travel problems. Yet all Collins could remember about the 1946 decision was that for years people had told him that taking the home-field advantage had been the wrong choice. So he gave the home-field advantage to the Giants!

This error in judgment played a critical role in deciding the 1951 pennant race. Thanks to Jack Collins' decision over his coin flip, the first playoff game of 1951 was played at Ebbets Field. The Dodgers lost, as Bobby Thomson hit a home run to center field. If the game had been played in the Polo Grounds, that ball would have stayed in the park and possibly been caught.

Then, in the third and deciding game, Thomson hit his historic home run to the short left-field porch in the Polo Grounds—a drive that would have almost certainly been caught at Ebbets Field.

If the Dodgers had made the logical decision on the coin flip, the ballparks would have been reversed, and Bobby Thomson would be just another name in *The Baseball Encyclopedia.*

The Bizarre
Baseball Craze of the 1880s

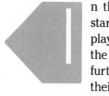n the early 1880s, the fad of the day was novelty baseball games. It started in 1880, when the hot summer weather inspired two teams to play a baseball game in the Hudson River just off the Albany Islands. All the infield play was in water up to the waist, and the outfielders were further out in the river where they floated and swam after the balls hit their way.

In 1882, the town of Buffalo had a series of games between teams known as the "Fats" and the "Leans." To play on the "Fat" team you had to weigh at least two hundred pounds. The "Lean" players, also known as the "Shadows," had to weigh under 140 pounds.

In the winter of 1883 you could find baseball played on ice skates in New York's Central Park. Runners were allowed to overslide the bases, which were ashes burned into the ice, and pitchers were forbidden to throw the dreaded "snowball."

There were hosts of other novelty teams, including women's clubs and several ethnic teams, one of which was all-Chinese and one made up entirely of American Indians. But the most unusual match of the era involved two teams called the Snorkies and the Hoppers.

A hazard of life in the 1880s was poor safety measures around the country's railroad yards. Thousands of people lost arms and legs slipping beneath the wheels of trains. Even a few major-league players suffered such accidents, including star catcher Charlie Bennett, who lost both his legs in a train accident.

In Washington, D.C., the Reading Railroad had an entire group of employees who had lost legs or were on crutches, and they formed a baseball team known as the "Hoppers."

Now, in 1883 there was an unusual pitcher named Hugh Daily with Cleveland in the National League. Daily pitched for six years in the major leagues despite the fact that his left arm was missing below the elbow. Impressed with the pluck of "One Arm" Daily, a group of similarly handicapped people formed a team in Philadelphia called the "Snorkies." Each Snorkey was either missing an arm or hand or had a paralyzed arm.

On May 23, 1883, the courageous Snorkies and Hoppers squared off in a battle for the cripple championship of the world. It was the kind of game where everyone was a winner, and no doubt Hugh Daily was pleased to hear that the Snorkies soundly beat the Hoppers by a score of 34-11.

Baseball's Legendary Indian Player

everal American Indians have had impressive major-league careers, including an all-Indian battery with the Athletics that included Hall of Fame pitcher Charles Bender and his catcher Chief Meyers. And the great Indian athlete Jim Thorpe was not only a football star but also played six years in the majors. Yet none of these fine athletes could approach the build-up given to Louis "Chief" Sockalexis, the first American Indian to play major-league baseball.

Sockalexis was a member of the Penobscot tribe in New England, the grandson of a tribal chief. Even though his brief major-league career touched only three seasons, he was a legendary player who captured the country's imagination back in the 1890s. He started as the dominant athlete in New England high school sports,

Louis "Chief" Sockalexis

including track and football as well as baseball.

Louis went on to play college baseball at Holy Cross and Notre Dame, where he reportedly accomplished a number of superhuman feats in both college and summer leagues. One of his homers was estimated at six hundred feet. He stole six bases in a single game and, in a contest against Harvard, he made a remarkable throw from the outfield that was measured at 414 feet on the fly.

In 1897, the manager of the Cleveland Spiders signed Sockalexis to a major-league contract after a single tryout. Sockalexis was an immediate star. By July he was hitting .338 with sixteen steals and an impressive eight triples in just sixty games. But Louis' season suddenly ground to a halt due to a drinking problem that had begun in his college days.

During a wild Fourth of July party in his rookie year, an inebriated Sockalexis fell from a second-story window and injured an ankle. Between the ankle injury and his heavy drinking, his major-league career was over almost before it started. He played just twenty-eight major-league games over the next two seasons, hitting only .236. His last game in the majors came when he was only twenty-seven years old.

Yet the immensity of Sockalexis' talent made such an impression on those who saw him play that he has been immortalized in both baseball and literature. A couple of years after Sockalexis' death in 1913, the Cleveland club in the American League held a contest to choose a new nickname. The fans remembered the great Indian player for the old Cleveland Spiders and chose to call the team the "Indians" in memory of Sockalexis.

Baseball researcher Jay Feldman discovered that Sockalexis also has a literary legacy, thanks to Gilbert Patten, who managed an opposing team when Sockalexis was starring in the New England summer leagues as a teenager. Patten, who wrote under the pen name Burt Standish, was so taken with the talents of Sockalexis that he used him as the model for the main character in a series of stories that made his fortune. The young Sockalexis was the original Frank Merriwell.

Harry Wright, Baseball's Greatest Pioneer

o man did more to advance professional baseball than Harry Wright. He was born in Sheffield, England, and brought to the United States by his father, a famous cricket bowler. Young Harry became one of the finest cricket players on this continent. In 1857, at age twenty-two, he played his first game of baseball and quickly became a star who once smashed seven homers in a single game.

In 1869, Harry organized the Cincinnati Red Stockings as baseball's first professional team. He was instrumental in forming the National Association, baseball's first professional league, and managed four pennant winners in five years. When the National League was formed in 1876, Harry began an eighteen-year managerial career that included thirteen winning seasons and two pennants.

Harry remained a progressive thinker throughout the years and developed many of baseball's basic strategies. Things like making defensive shifts against the batter, pitchers backing up the bases, the catcher using hand signals, the hidden ball trick, and double steals—all these originated on teams managed by Harry. In 1870, his catcher became the first player to wear a glove, and in 1875, Harry introduced the catcher's mask to the major leagues.

Harry was a true gentleman who abstained from tobacco, alcohol, and profanity, and was modest to a fault. In his later years he quietly rejected references to himself as the "Father of the Game." Despite his interest in turning baseball into a professional sport, which put a heavy emphasis on winning, he was a firm believer in honest sportsmanship. One time in Cincinnati he overruled a hometown umpire he felt had made an unfair call against the visiting team. Although it ultimately cost him the game, he called his own player out and removed him from the field.

Harry's character established a baseball precedent for all time. In 1869, Harry's Red Stockings had toured the country playing all the top teams in the land and gone undefeated in sixty-six games. In 1870, the Cincinnati club had extended its streak to an unbelievable 84 games when they found themselves tied after nine innings with the Brooklyn Atlantics. As was the general practice of the day, the Atlantics wanted to call it a draw, but Harry refused to allow the streak to end on a tie—insisting it be win or lose. And in the eleventh inning, his team finally lost, 8-7.

Yet Harry Wright had established a central principle in the game of baseball. Whenever the conditions permit, the game is played to a conclusion. The next time your team goes into extra innings, think of Harry Wright—and his club's eighty-four-game winning streak.

Eddie Plank, the Unluckiest Pitcher in World Series History

E ddie Plank of the Philadelphia Athletics won 327 regular-season games, but come World Series time, he was a steady loser to lady luck.

It was luck that matched Plank's first World Series start against Christy Mathewson in the opening game of the 1905 Series. That happened to be the year Mathewson threw his famous three shutouts, and Plank was his first victim, 3-0.

Eddie drew a second start in that Series and was matched with another Hall of Famer, Iron Man McGinnity. Plank pitched brilliantly, allowing only four hits, but a couple of errors allowed a run to score, and Plank lost 1-0 on an unearned run. For the Series, he ended up 0-2, despite a 1.59 ERA.

In 1911, Plank got into his second World Series, and the Athletics finally scored their first runs for him as he beat Hall of Famer Rube Marquard on a five-hitter, 3-1. But Plank also got stuck with another loss, when he allowed a run in a rare relief appearance in the fifth game.

In his next World Series, in 1913, he again found himself pitching against

Eddie Plank

Mathewson. Plank was impressive and had a shutout through nine innings. Unfortunately, so did Christy, and the Giants broke through in the tenth inning to defeat Plank. Eddie finally beat Mathewson in the finale game, but it took a brilliant two-hitter to do it.

1914 was Plank's fourth and final World Series appearance. Bill James of the Boston Braves matched him 0 for 0 for eight innings. Plank, who was thirty-nine years old at the time, tired in the ninth and allowed a single run, to lose 1-0.

Although Plank had pitched brilliantly in four different series, he retired with only two World Series wins and five losses—the second-most losses in World Series history.

Plank's World Series Record	W-L	ERA
1905	0-2	1.59
1911	1-1	1.86
1913	1-1	0.95
1914	0-1	1.00
TOTAL	2-5	1.32

With an overall ERA of 1.32 and an average of fewer than six hits and two walks for every nine innings, how in the world did Plank go 2-5 in World Series competition?

First, he was constantly matched with some of the best pitchers in baseball history. Five of his six World Series starts were against Hall of Famers at the peak of their careers. The only non-Hall of Fame opponent was Bill James, and he was coming off a career year in which he was as good as or better than most Hall of Famers.

Regular Season Record of Opposing W.S. Starter		
1905 Mathewson	31-8	1.27
1905 McGinnity	21-15	2.87
1911 Marquard	24-7	2.50
1913 Mathewson	25-11	2.06
1913 Mathewson	25-11	2.06
1914 James	26-7	1.90
Average	25-10	2.11

Still, Plank should have sued the Athletic hitters for non-support. With Eddie on the mound they scored less than a run every nine innings. They were shut out in four of his six starts and, to Plank's credit, he won the only two times his team scored for him.

The rule is, "You can't win if you can't score," and not even Eddie Plank could break that rule.

The Three Shots of Rye

ene Rye's real name was Eugene Mercantelli. Why he chose the name Rye for his baseball career remains a mystery, but his nickname of "Half-Pint" was a natural. The Boston outfielder stood only five-feet-six.

Rye did his best hitting as a minor leaguer in the Texas League. There he compiled a career .319 average, and in 1930 he connected for twenty-six homers with 92 RBIs. The next season, he got his only trial in the big leagues, but in the big show he was an absolute bust. In thirty-nine at bats with the 1931 Red Sox he collected only seven hits, all singles, for a .179 batting average.

Half-Pint Rye's real claim to fame is the game that brought him to the attention of the Red Sox. On August 6, 1930, the team from Waco crushed Beaumont 22-4 in a Texas League game. It was actually a close game until the eighth inning, but then the Waco club set a record by scoring eighteen runs in a single inning. The star of the eighth was none other than Gene Half-Pint Rye.

Gene led off the historic inning by pulling a ball into the right-field seats, but it went foul by a couple of feet. Rye then hit the next pitch to the opposite field for a home run. When the team had batted around and he found himself facing a new pitcher with two men on, Rye hit another home run.

Incredibly, Waco kept hitting and Rye got up in the inning a third time. This time the bases were loaded. Yes, Half-Pint Rye hit a grand slam for this third homer in the *inning*. He set four professional baseball records for one inning: most total bases (12), most extra bases (9), most RBIs (8) and most home runs (3), all records that probably will never be broken.

Baseball's Ambidextrous Pitchers

The idea of a pitcher throwing both left-handed and right-handed in a major-league game is not as far-fetched as most fans think. A number of major-league players in this century have demonstrated an ability to throw with either hand.

Hank Grampp, a batting-practice pitcher in the 1930s, used to do it. In the 1940s, infielder Jackie Price and catcher Paul Richards had the ability to throw with either hand. In fact, in a high-school game Richards had actually pitched as both a righty and a lefty. In the modern era, relief pitcher Greg Harris often throws both right- and left-handed on the sidelines, and even has a special fielding glove that he can switch from one hand to the other.

Yet we have now gone for more than a hundred years without a pitcher's having switched arms in a major-league game, although baseball researcher Al Kermisch has discovered that prior to 1889, no less than three pitchers performed this feat.

The first ambidextrous pitcher in the major leagues was star "right-hander" Tony Mullane. Back in the 1880s, Mullane was particularly proud of his ambidexterity. He often threw both lefty and righty on the sidelines, and he created a sensation as one of the earliest switch-hitters.

On July 18, 1882, Mullane tried pitching lefty in an actual game, switching to his left hand in the fourth inning of a contest with Baltimore. He retired all three batters, all of whom were batting left-handed. Accounts of the game are unclear as to whether Mullane continued to pitch as a lefty for the rest of the game, but he did lose the game on a home run by a left-handed batter. Mullane is the only switch-pitcher recognized in *The Baseball Encyclopedia,* where his listing reads "Bats: Both, Throws: Both."

On June 16, 1884, Larry Corcoran of Chicago became a reluctant switch-pitcher. The only pitcher his team had available that day, Cocoran opened an ugly blister on his right index finger and gamely tried to continue by throwing left-handed. He didn't last long, and two infielders and an outfielder had to finish the second half of a 20-9 defeat.

The third ambidextrous pitcher was Elton "Icebox" Chamberlain. On May 10, 1888, he defeated Kansas City 18-6, and in the last two innings the right-hander switched arms and threw a lefty. He allowed four hits and no runs.

It appears that Icebox Chamberlain was the only pitcher who switched in a winning effort, and probably the only pitcher to be unscored on from his unnatural side. Yet for all his success he was the last of this unusual breed.

Elton "Icebox" Chamberlain with St. Louis in 1889.

Baseball's Most Frustrated Hitter

ost of baseball's lousiest hitters have been pitchers who didn't really care about hitting. Tiger pitcher Hank Aguirre was an exception—he really cared about his hitting and tried like crazy to erase his image as the worst hitter in baseball.

Aguirre pitched sixteen years in the majors from 1955 to 1970. In 388 career at bats, he struck out more than *two-thirds* of the time. He never hit a home run and finished with a career average of .085. What makes his story so incredible is that he had to make a significant improvement to get his average that high.

In his first seven seasons, Aguirre tried everything he could think of to improve as a hitter. He took extra batting practice, studied books and films, and took all the batting advice he could get. In 1962, Aguirre found himself approaching mid-season without a single hit. His career batting average had fallen near .050. On June 22, 1962, it dawned on Aguirre that he was a left-handed pitcher but he swung the bat right-handed.

Then and there Aguirre decided to become a left-handed hitter. In his next at bat, on the first official left-handed swing of his life, he hit a soft drive to right field that fell for an RBI single. The hometown crowd of 44,000 Tiger fans gave Aguirre a standing ovation.

Aguirre was convinced that he had solved his problem; he had simply been batting from the wrong side his whole life. Hank got only one more hit in the 1962 season to go 2 for 75, an .027 average, but Aguirre wasn't discouraged. He continued to work at his hitting and even tried switch-hitting for a few seasons.

In the loosest sense of the word, Aguirre was a better hitter the last half of his career. He blistered the ball at a .132 clip the next year and averaged .106 over his last eight seasons. Not bad when you consider that .106 is exactly twice his .053 average for the first eight seasons. It's doubtful any other hitter in baseball history can match his 100 percent improvement.

Hank Aguirre proved that anyone can learn to hit—at least a little.

The Hall of Fame Iron Man

verything about Joe McGinnity suggested a durable toughness. He was born in Rock Island, Illinois, he packed over 200 pounds on his five-foot-eleven frame, and in the off-season he worked in his father-in-law's iron foundry, which is where he got the nickname "Iron Man."

At age twenty-eight, the submarine curveballer was a late arrival in the major leagues in 1899, but his presence was felt immediately. He led the league in both wins and innings pitched in both his rookie and sophomore seasons. He began his career with a streak of eight straight seasons with over 20 wins and led the league five times each in wins and innings pitched.

In 1903 he won 31 games at age thirty-two, making him the only man in baseball history to win 30 games after age thirty. Then for good measure he did it again the next year, but this time with 35 wins and a league leading 1.61 ERA! He also threw over 400 innings in both seasons, a unique feat even in that era. His 434 innings in 1903 remains the National League record for this century.

Iron Man McGinnity left the Giants in 1909 due to a dispute with manager John McGraw. The thirty-nine-year-old Iron Man felt that McGraw had lost confidence in his durability and was trying to put him out to pasture as a starter-reliever. In 1908,

Joe "Iron Man"
McGinnity

McGraw had used him seventeen times in relief and only twenty times as a starter. McGinnity had led in relief wins and was third in saves, but McGinnity wanted to return to the role of a workhorse starter.

Joe had jumped teams twice before in his career, and this time he jumped to the Newark club in the Eastern League when they assured him a job as their number one starter. The Iron Man was back in true form, throwing over 400 innings in each of his first two seasons while also leading in wins with 29 and 30.

In 1913, McGinnity went out west and threw a personal high of *436* innings for Tacoma in the Northwestern League. He was forty-two years old at the time. In 1915, at age forty-four, he still led the league in innings pitched with 355.

The Iron Man finally quit after the 1925 season when he was only 6-6 for Dubuque in the Mississippi Valley League. Of course, by then he was fifty-four years old. In butting heads with the Iron Man, John McGraw was far from a genius. McGinnity ended up winning more than 200 games after their argument over his declining durability as a starting pitcher.

Smoke Justice, Four No-Hitters in One Season!

f you go by his listing in *The Baseball Enclyclopedia*, Walter "Smoke" Justice is just another obscure and insignificant pitcher. We know that he pitched briefly for the Detroit Tigers in 1905 when he was just twenty-one years old. His entire major-league career consisted of two undistinguished relief appearances. He had control problems as he walked six batters in just 3⅓ innings, finishing with an ERA of 8.10.

But Smoke Justice continued to pitch in the minors long after his brief major-league career. In 1907, he won 22 games for Lancaster in the Ohio State League, including an eighteen-inning shutout that he won 1-0. As his nickname suggests, Smoke Justice was a fastball pitcher. In 1908, at the height of the Dead-Ball Era, when strikeouts came few and far between, Justice struck out 293 batters and won a career-high 25 games.

That same 1908 season gave Smoke Justice a unique page in baseball's record books. No-hitters, whether in the major or minor leagues, are a rare event usually requiring a dash of luck as well as overwhelming talent. In over 100 years of baseball no major leaguer has had more than two no-hitters in a season. A couple of minor leaguers have managed three in a season, but only one has tossed four zeros in the hit column in a single season.

At age twenty-four, Justice threw a no-hitter on July 19, 1908. Just eleven days later, he threw a second no-hitter. About a month after that, he came up with a third no-hitter, and a week later on September 13 he made history by throwing his fourth no-hitter.

Not only did he record four no-hitters in a single season, but he bunched them in a span of less than two months. All four were clean performances with no unearned runs and no questionable scoring calls. In the four games, Justice averaged two walks and ten strikeouts; no runner got past second, and only fourteen balls were hit out of the infield.

Oddly enough, there is no record of Justice ever throwing another no-hitter, and he struggled when he advanced to the higher leagues. Yet his four no-hitters in fifty-seven days remains an amazing part of minor-league history.

Wee Willie Keeler and his Famous Hitting Streak

illie Keeler, the Hall of Famer who "hit 'em where they ain't," was an outstanding player even though he was under five-feet-five and weighed only 140 pounds. The speedy Baltimore outfielder was a master bunter, an adept batsman on the hit-and-run, and the inventor of the Baltimore chop. In a nineteen-year career that stretched from 1892 to 1910, he hit over .300 in fifteen consecutive seasons, had eight straight seasons of 200 hits or more, and retired with a .345 batting average, the highest of any hitter who played his entire career in the Dead-Ball Era.

Wee Willie Keeler

In 1897, the twenty-five-year-old Keeler collected a hit in 44 consecutive games, a remarkable feat that stood for 44 years until broken by Joe DiMaggio in 1941. It remained the undisputed National League record for over 80 years until Pete Rose tied it in 1978.

After the streak was over, Keeler set another record by collecting *fourteen* hits in a span of three consecutive games. That's the major-league record under the modern pitching distance of sixty feet, six inches. Considering the two record-setting feats, it is no surprise that 1897 was the best season of Keeler's career. He took the batting title with a .432 mark, the third-highest average in all of major-league history.

Although Keeler's hitting streak has been surpassed in length, in other ways it remains unique. His 44-game batting streak is special in that it began with two hits on *Opening Day* of the 1897 season. His streak holds a 10-game edge as the longest hitting streak ever to begin a season.

Keeler's hitting streak also stands out from that of Joe DiMaggio, and so many others, in the number of hits Willie collected during the streak. The vast majority of Keeler's games were multiple-hit games. In 20 percent of the games he had three hits or more. Only 36 percent of his games kept the streak alive with a single hit. By contrast, more than 60 percent of the games in DiMaggio's streak involved a single hit.

The Most Controversial
Catch in World Series History

One of baseball's most disputed plays occurred in the 1925 World Series between the Pittsburgh Pirates and Washington Senators. A key figure in the Series and in this play was Hall of Fame outfielder Sam Rice. Sam hit .364 in the Series and collected twelve hits, which stood as the World Series record for thirty-nine years before being broken by Bobby Richardson. But Rice's hitting was overshadowed by the catch he did—or did not—make on October 10, 1925.

With the Series tied at one game each, the Senators led 4-3 in the eighth inning of the third game. Pirate catcher Earl Smith hit a long drive to right center field where temporary bleachers had been set up to handle the overflow crowd. Rice, considered the best defensive right fielder in the league, raced toward the barrier to intercept what looked to be a game-tying home run. Rice leaped up for the ball, appeared to catch it, and then toppled into the stands.

Rice was completely out of view for at least ten seconds before reemerging with the ball in his glove. Umpire Cy Rigler called Smith out, and the Pirates stormed the field, protesting the call. Pirates' owner Barney Dreyfuss appealed to Commissioner Landis, who stopped the game and had Rice brought over to his box. When asked if he caught it, Rice simply replied, "The umpire said I did."

The play stood and the Senators won the game, 4-3. For the rest of his life Rice stuck to his answer that the umpire said he'd made the catch. But in 1965, he gave the Hall of Fame a letter to be opened after his death. He claimed the letter had the true story of the catch.

Rice's wishes were respected and the letter was not opened until after his death in 1974. The letter made it clear that Sam simply enjoyed fanning the flame of controversy over the play that made him famous. His constant reference to the umpire's call suggested he might not have hung onto the ball when he fell into the stands. But the letter he left behind stated clearly his belief that he caught the ball and that "at no time did I lose possession of the ball."

That was literally the last word on the most controversial play in World Series history.

The Trivia Catcher

oe "Gabber" Glenn had changed his last name from Gurzensky to make it easier to remember. That seemed like a good idea considering that he would have what looks, on the surface, like a faceless career. He played eight years in the majors, most of them as Bill Dickey's backup in the 1930s. He averaged less than ninety at bats a season and hit a boring .252.

Yet somehow Glenn was behind the plate for three of that era's most interesting pitching moments. The first occurred on the last day of the 1933 season. Babe Ruth

Joe "Gabber" Glenn

made his final pitching appearance in the majors, going all the way in a complete game victory. Behind the plate was twenty-four-year-old Joe Glenn, catching only the tenth game in his major-league career.

Bill Dickey caught over 1,700 games in *his* major-league career, yet not one was a no-hitter. From 1918 to 1950, a span of thirty-three years, Monte Pearson was the only Yankee pitcher to hurl a no-hitter. That no-hit gem occurred on August 27, 1937, and, yes, Joe Glenn—who caught only twenty-four games that year—was calling the pitches.

Glenn's next brush with baseball history came in his final big-league season. In 1940, Joe Glenn was traded to the Boston Red Sox, where he hit only .128 and caught in only nineteen games, but was once again behind the plate when history was made.

On August 24, the Detroit Tigers were blasting the Red Sox. Glenn was put behind the plate to give the starting catcher a rest, and Hall of Famer Ted Williams came in from left field to pitch two innings. Pitching to the capable hands of the last man to catch Babe Ruth, Ted allowed one run in two innings and struck out Rudy York on three pitches.

Joe Glenn caught only 235 games in the majors, but he managed to catch a rare Yankee no-hitter, Babe Ruth's last game, and Ted Williams in his only major-league pitching appearance. You won't find Joe Glenn's name next to any major-league records, but it does come up as the answer to a lot of trivia questions.

Baseball's First Superstar

im Creighton was a young wizard of a pitcher who starred for the Brooklyn Excelsiors, possibly the best of baseball's pre-Civil War teams. Creighton's secret was delivery that used a special snap of the wrist. It was so effective that a rule change was later adopted, requiring pitchers to deliver the ball with a stiff wrist.

Although professional baseball was still a decade away, Creighton is often referred to as the game's first professional player. Popular history states that the Excelsiors paid the youngster a modest salary to keep him from jumping to another athletic club.

Creighton was recognized as an exceptional athlete in every regard—a fine hitter, runner, and fielder. On July 22, 1860, he was playing in left field when he charged an apparent hit, made a spectacular one-handed catch, and made a powerful throw that started the first triple play ever recorded in the New York newspapers.

In 1861, Creighton and his Excelsiors claimed they were twice as good as any other team in the New York area. On September 21, they played their nine-man team against an eighteen-man team—the best from the New York clubs. In addition to giving them nine extra men in the field, the Excelsiors also allowed their opponents six outs an inning. Yet Jim Creighton and the Excelsiors still won the game, 45-16.

The Excelsiors remained a star team for many years. Researcher John Thorn notes that in 1869 they played what was probably the first "old-timers game." An exhibition game was scheduled between the 1869 squad and the famous 1859 Excelsiors—who had to play without their most famous member. Jim Creighton had been mortally wounded on the diamond seven years earlier.

In a game against the Unions of Morrisania, Creighton hit a home run. But on the swing, he ruptured his bladder. That injury caused his death on October 18, 1862, according to the *Brooklyn Eagle*. Baseball's first superstar was a victim of the game just five months short of his twenty-second birthday.

The Self-Made Hall of Famer

Maximilian Carnarius set out to be a Lutheran minister but went on to baseball fame under the name of Max Carey. He got his first tryout by showing a minor-league manager a track medal he had earned as a sprinter. Carey hit only .158 that first pro season, but he was determined to succeed in his new calling. He taught himself to switch-hit, and by 1910 he was hitting .293 when the Pittsburgh Pirates purchased his contract.

Carey continued to work on his game throughout his major-league career. Hall of Fame teammate Honus Wagner worked with him on conditioning his legs and reading the pitcher's move to first base. Carey eventually led the league in stolen

Max Carey

bases for ten seasons, still the all-time record. His success rate on the bases was phenomenal. In 1922, he stole fifty-one bases and was caught only *twice*, a 96 percent success rate.

Although Carey is best known for his base stealing, he worked hard in every area to become the most valuable player he could be. To make himself a better leadoff hitter, Max gradually became a master at drawing walks and twice led the league in free passes.

Defensively, Max became one of the greatest center fielders of all time. Nine times he led the league in outfield catches—still the major-league record—and his 339 outfield assists are the most of any National League outfielder in this century.

Carey believed a dog was never too old to learn new tricks. At age thirty-four, he totally remodeled his stance after seeing Ty Cobb hit in an exhibition game. The next year, Carey hit .343, the best mark of his career. That same year Max got into the only World Series of his career, and his studious approach helped the Pirates win the deciding game of the Series.

The Pirates' opponents in the 1925 World Series were Walter Johnson and the Washington Senators. The Big Train had already beaten the Pirates twice, 4-1 and 4-0, before taking the mound for the seventh and deciding game.

This time Carey was ready for him. 1925 was Walter Johnson's last big year, and the thirty-eight-year-old fireballer was mixing in a looping curveball with his normal fastballs. Max discovered that Johnson was tipping off his curveball by shortening up his delivery. Armed with this knowledge, the Pirates came back from a 4-0 deficit to beat Johnson and the Senators 9-7. Carey led the Pirate attack with four hits, including three doubles and a stolen base.

Max Carey, the self-made Hall of Famer, became a self-made World Champion as well.

The World Series of Pitching

he 1905 World Series was expected to be a high-scoring Series between the Philadelphia Athletics and the New York Giants. Both teams had led their league in runs scored, and the Athletics' best pitcher, Rube Waddell, was not available for the Series because of a shoulder injury incurred during some horseplay with a teammate.

The Series opened in Philadelphia as the Giants' Christy Mathewson blanked the A's on a four-hitter, 3-0. That looked familiar the next day as Chief Bender returned the favor by beating the Giants by the same 3-0 score and also allowed only four hits. It was a tough loss for the Giants' Iron Man McGinnity as all three Philadelphia runs resulted from a couple of fielding errors.

A rainout allowed Mathewson to come back and pitch game 3, and again he blanked the A's on four hits and won easily 9-0. Then in game 4, McGinnity and Eddie Plank got into a classic pitcher's duel that was settled 1-0 on an unearned run. This time McGinnity came away the winner as A's third baseman Lave Cross made the crucial error.

When Mathewson had beaten the A's 9-0 back in the third game, the Giants had staked him to a two-run lead in the first and expanded it to seven runs by the fifth inning. Mathewson had coasted the rest of the game and now felt so strong that he went to manager John McGraw and said he was ready to pitch on just one day's rest. McGraw agreed, and again Mathewson whitewashed the Athletics, this time on six hits, for a 2-0 victory to clinch the Giants' world championship.

Never before or since has quality pitching so totally smothered two excellent offensive teams. Consider these three stunning facts:

1) Every game was won by a shutout.
2) In two of the games not a single earned run by either team crossed the plate.
3) The Giants' ERA for the Series was a perfect 0.00.

In looking back at the quality of the pitchers involved, the outcome was less surprising. Both teams started Hall of Fame pitchers in every game with the exception of Philadelphia in game 3. Those pitchers combined for 79 innings and allowed only 5 earned runs, an ERA of 0.57.

Christy Mathewson's performance was the real model of efficiency. In his 27 innings he allowed only 14 hits and a single walk. His three shutouts in a single Series have never been matched. In fact, Christy Mathewson is the *only* ballplayer who ever pitched more than three World Series shutouts.

Life Begins at 40

ife begins at forty? Not in baseball—unless your name happens to be Earl Caldwell. This lanky right-hander from Sparks, Texas, made his major-league debut with the 1928 Phillies at age twenty-three, but a 5.71 ERA quickly sent him back to the minors. He resurfaced seven years later with the St. Louis Browns, but after three mediocre seasons he was cut loose again at age thirty-three.

No one expected to see Caldwell in the majors again, but he continued to hang on in the minors and, eight years later in 1945, the Chicago White Sox added him to their war-torn roster. Despite being forty years old, he was impressive enough that the Chicago club asked him back in 1946 even though their regular players were returning from the war.

Caldwell had no trouble earning his place on the team and becoming the best relief pitcher in the American League. He had an excellent ERA of 2.08; he was also second in saves and first in relief wins, with thirteen victories against only four defeats.

Caldwell's teammates considered him a second pitching coach and nicknamed him "Teach." He remained in the majors for another two seasons and won his last major-league game in 1948 at age 43—exactly twenty years after his first major-league appearance.

But Earl Caldwell's success in his twilight years did not end there. He returned to the minors at age forty-four and just kept on pitching, finishing his professional career with six straight seasons in which his ERA was under 2.90.

At age forty-six, he led the Gulf Coast League in ERA. Incredibly, it was his first

Earl Caldwell

ERA title in any league, in a career that had already spanned twenty-six seasons. He then went on to lead his league in ERA for three straight years, from ages forty-six to forty-eight.

Caldwell's 1953 season probably meant more to him than any of his twenty-nine professional seasons, including his eight years in the majors. The forty-eight-year-old not only led the Evangeline League with a 2.07 ERA, but did it with a very special battery mate. His catcher that season was his son, Earl Caldwell, Jr.

The Timing of the Fastball

or the first eighty years of baseball history, people could only guess at how fast a pitcher could throw a baseball. The first estimates compared the speed to that of the fastest trains, and even in the 1900s that was around one hundred miles per hour. It was this comparison that led to famed fireballer Walter Johnson's nickname "The Big Train."

As recently as the early 1940s, attempts to measure the speed of a fastball were so primitive that they involved having a pitcher try to release his throw at the exact moment a motorcycle went by at a set speed.

The first truly accurate timing of the fastball came in 1946, thanks to technology developed during World War II. Not far from Washington, D.C., in Aberdeen, Maryland, was a munitions company that tested the speeds of various artillery shells. The device they had developed for that purpose used a very accurate photoelectric cell, and they made it available to the Washington Senators prior to a game in May of 1946. The Cleveland Indians were in town with their star attraction, Bob Feller, considered the fastest pitcher in baseball at the time.

Prior to the game, Feller threw thirty to forty pitches through the measuring device set up over home plate. Later, Feller had reason to regret his part in the experiment. The scheduled game went into extra innings before Feller lost by a score of 2-1. He probably wished he had saved some of the pitches he fired through the speed machine, particularly the one measured at 98.6 miles per hour.

Today, pitchers' fastballs are measured by the same kind of radar devices used by the police to identify speeding motorists. This practice began with college coach Danny Litwhiler at Michigan State University, and Earl Weaver brought the idea to the major leagues. The fastest pitchers are lucky to get up in the mid-90s on these radar guns. When Feller indoctrinated baseball into the speedometer world of fastballs, his ability to throw a 98.6 fastball on that given day was truly exceptional.

Of all the hundreds of thousands of pitches recorded in the modern era, the fastest was thrown by Nolan Ryan of the California Angels on September 7, 1974, in a game against the White Sox. The official clocking was 100.8 miles per hour!

MVPs Who Weren't Winners

here seems an unwritten rule that the Most Valuable Player award must go to a player from a winning club—unless he plays for the Chicago Cubs. This exception began in 1952, when the voters rejected 28-game winner Robin Roberts as a candidate, and none of the winning teams had an outstanding performance from an everyday player. The pennant-winning Dodgers had won with a bunch of guys having good seasons, but no one was great. No pitcher won more than fifteen games, no regular hit higher than .308, and although Gil Hodges led the club with thirty-two homers he hit only .254. Among the other contenders, the best season belonged to Stan Musial. He captured the batting title with a .336 mark, but he hit only twenty-one homers with 91 RBIs.

The voters finally found their MVP on the fifth-place Cubs—left fielder Hank Sauer, who had led the league with thirty-seven homers and 121 RBIs. Despite Sauer's heroics, the Cubs posted a .500 record, which made Sauer the first MVP not to play on a winning team.

Six years later, another Cub player became the first MVP to come from a losing club. In 1958, there was no question about who was the National League's Most

Hank Sauer (left) with Ralph Kiner in 1953.

Valuable Player. He collected twenty more RBIs than any other player in the league. He took the home run crown by a margin of twelve, and for good measure he hit .313. To top it all off, this awesome hitting performance came from a shortstop. Ernie Banks was named MVP despite having played for a Cubs team that came in ten games below .500.

Once the voters accepted that an MVP could come from a losing team, it was easy

for them to give it to Banks again the very next year when he led the league with 143 RBIs. And again the Cubs managed to lose more than they won.

Then, twenty-nine years later, the Cubs broke new ground when right fielder Andre Dawson was voted the league's Most Valuable Player after leading the league with forty-seven homers and 137 RBIs. He is the only player to win the MVP award while playing for a *last place* team.

Tommy "The Limey" Brown and the Lord Baltimores

The American Association was originally classified as a major league and was in open competition with the National League from 1882 to 1891. Their team in Maryland was known as the Lord Baltimores, and they were a typical nineteenth-century ballclub.

The Lord Baltimores were not usually a rowdy lot, but in September of 1883, Baltimore manager Bill Barney was faced with two of the most common problems afflicting baseball in the 1800s—alcohol and the difficulty of maneuvering with a small roster of about fifteen players.

On the evening of September 3, several of the Lord Baltimores—including the entire three-man pitching staff—attended a masked ball at the Kernan Hotel. This would not have been a problem had they not been scheduled to play Columbus the very next afternoon. The players drank themselves into a stupor, and Hardy Henderson, the scheduled starting pitcher, spent the night in jail after taking part in a street brawl.

The next afternoon, the manager took one look at his hungover crew and socked Henderson and catcher John Sweeney with $100 fines. Several others were fined $10 for attending the masked ball and being out too late. However, with the team's small roster, Barney had no choice but to use the offenders in that day's game.

As you might have guessed, Columbus swamped Baltimore 21-4. Henderson lasted only three innings, giving up nine runs. His fellow pitcher and drinking buddy, Bob Emsley, also failed to finish the game in relief. Gid Gardner, an outfielder, had to be pressed into pitching duty to complete the farce of a game.

Where does Tommy Brown fit into all this? Tommy "The Limey" Brown—originally a native of Liverpool, England—was the right fielder for the Columbus team that beat the tar out of the handicapped Lord Baltimores. Brown was a pretty decent player who played 17 years in the major leagues, but never had a better day at the plate. He hit the ball as hard as the Lord Baltimores had hit the bar the night before. The newspaper accounts show that Brown went six for six, including two doubles and two home runs.

Yet somehow Brown has never been credited in the record books with his rare performance. To this day, Brown is missing from the official list of major leaguers who have gone six for six in a single game. Perhaps the record keeper had been out celebrating with the Lord Baltimores the night before.

The First World Series

he fall classic began on a sunny afternoon on October 1, 1903. The National League champions, the Pittsburgh Pirates, took on the American League champs, the Boston Pilgrims—forerunners of the Red Sox—in a nine-game series to determine a "world champion."

The Pilgrims played in a freakish ballpark with a mammoth center-field area, the largest of any major-league park in history. The deepest part of the field was 635 feet from home plate. The series became the Grand Prix of triples. Where no other World Series has produced more than ten three-baggers, the 1903 Series saw sixteen triples by Boston alone, and twenty-five by the two teams combined. Pittsburgh's Tommy Leach ran out four triples, and that remains the *career* record for World Series play.

The Pilgrims won the Series in eight games, led by Hall of Fame pitcher Cy Young, who had a 1.59 ERA, and pitcher Bill Dineen, who won three games, including a four-hit shutout in the deciding game.

The total attendance for the Series was around 100,000, which wasn't bad considering neither park could hold much more than 18,000. Also holding down attendance was a 100 percent markup in the price of a ticket—fifty cents compared to the regular-season admission of twenty-five cents. The winner's share was worth $1,182 to each Boston Pilgrim. Odly enough, the Pirate players got about $150 more per man than the winners.

The 1903 Pirates went into the first World Series short-handed and with injuries to both their best pitcher and best player. Their most valuable player, shortstop Honus Wagner, had injured his right leg at the end of the season, and some thought he would skip the Series, which in some eyes was nothing more than a glorified exhibition match. But Wagner went ahead and played every game despite a noticeable limp.

The Pirates' best pitcher was Sam Leever, who had led the league in ERA. But Leever had a shoulder injury suffered in a trap-shooting tournament just after the end of the season. He lasted only one inning in his first start and gave up six runs in his second game.

Making things even tougher on the pitching was the tragic case of Ed Doheny. During the regular season the nine-year veteran had won 16 games against only eight losses, but he finally succumbed to a long battle with mental illness and had to be institutionalized prior to the Series.

Despite these handicaps, the Pirates played so gamely that club owner Barney Dreyfuss donated his share of the profits to his players. That amounted to approximately $5,000 and explains why the losing players actually received more money from the first World Series than the winners!

In a historical sense, the Pirates earned it. Rather than taking the easy way out by treating the Series as a lark, they began the tradition that the World Series would be a true competition. Without their serious and earnest play, the Series would have had the same circus atmosphere as earlier "championship series" and almost certainly faded away.

A game in Boston during the first World Series in 1903.

Baseball's
Human Good-Luck Charm

harlie "Victory" Faust was twenty-nine years old when, in the summer of 1911, he had a fateful meeting with a fortune teller at a fair in Wichita, Kansas. The seer told Faust that he would pitch the New York Giants to a pennant, so naturally Charlie headed for St. Louis where he could meet up with the Giants, who were scheduled to play the Cardinals.

Giants manager John McGraw had a strong superstitious streak, and when he heard Faust's story, he agreed to give him a personal tryout. It turned out that Charlie couldn't throw the ball any harder than a child. At one point McGraw threw away his glove and caught Faust barehanded. Just for kicks, McGraw put Faust in a Giant uniform and let him watch as the Giants beat the Cardinals 8-0. That was supposed to be the end of it, but Faust wouldn't give up. He didn't have enough money to take the train, so he joined the hobos in riding the rails all the way from St. Louis to New York.

Faust became the Giants mascot and quickly became a fan favorite with his pre-game antics. The players liked him because he really did seem to bring them luck. Whenever the Giants fell behind, McGraw would warm Charlie up in the bullpen and, almost magically, the Giants would stage a comeback.

At one point, Faust left the club to appear in vaudeville, but when the Giants went into an extended losing streak he jumped his contract to return to the team. When Charlie Faust rejoined the Giants, they got hot again and won their first pennant in six years. After clinching the pennant McGraw completed the prophecy by placing Faust on the active roster and actually letting him pitch an inning in a couple of games. For the record, Faust allowed two hits and one run for an ERA of 4.50.

But the fortune teller predicted nothing beyond a pennant. The Giants lost the World Series, and the next year Faust was only allowed to sit on the team bench in his street clothes. They won the pennant again, but they barred Faust from the World Series in hopes of avoiding the previous year's fate. It didn't help; they lost the Series again, and they lost Faust who packed his bags and headed for California.

Without Faust, the Giants won two fewer games. The next year they dropped seventeen more in the win column. Out on the West Coast, Faust contracted tuberculosis and died in the middle of the 1915 baseball season.

And the Giants? They finished last that year, their first losing record in thirteen years.

Stuffy McInnis and Baseball's Most Unusual Home Run

 ohn "Stuffy" McInnis joined the Philadelphia Athletics in 1909 as a slick-fielding shortstop, but the Athletics were blessed with the three best infielders in the league. Frank "Home Run" Baker was at third base, Jack Barry was at shortstop, and Eddie Collins anchored second base. When McInnis became their regular first baseman in 1911, he set in place what many consider the best defensive infield in the history of the game.

The former shortstop went on to become possibly the greatest defensive first baseman of all time. Because of improvements in gloves and the care of fields since those days, no player from the Dead-Ball Era (prior to 1920) ranks among the least error-prone at his position—with the exception of Stuffy McInnis.

Stuffy retired with a slew of fielding records, many of which still stand today, over seventy years later. He is the only first baseman to handle over 1,500 chances in a season and make only one error. And he still holds the major-league record of 1,700 consecutive chances at first base without an error.

McInnis was also an impressive contact hitter. He ranks as the sixth toughest batter to strike out in baseball history. He hit over .300 twelve times and helped lead the Athletics to five pennants in his nineteen-year career. One thing McInnis was not, though, was a home run hitter. He never hit more than 4 in a season and had only 20 for his whole career, but one of those homers brought about a change in the rule book.

In 1911, the rules did not provide for pitchers to throw warm-up pitches at the start of an inning, although the pitcher usually got in a few tosses before the leadoff

Stuffy McInnis

batter stepped in. One day, in a game against the Red Sox, Stuffy McInnis was in the field and realized he would be leading off in the seventh inning. At the end of the sixth inning, he rushed to the dugout to get his bat and walked briskly to the plate. Boston pitcher Ed Kargar released an easy warm-up toss and Stuffy jumped into the batter's box and hit a soft fly to the outfield.

But it was an empty outfield, as the Boston players were still trotting out to their positions. McInnis circled the bases and the umpire called him safe, explaining, "He hit from the batter's box, the pitcher was on the rubber, the catcher was in his box, and time was not called. That's a home run."

The very next year the rule book provided for the pitcher to take eight warm-up throws in one minute before each inning started. Pitchers everywhere can thank Stuffy McInnis for making it official.

What's the Color of Your Sox?

n 1882, William Hulbert served simultaneously as both the president of the National League and the owner of the league's Chicago franchise. The manager of his team was Al Spalding, the Hall of Fame pitcher who also owned a successful sporting goods company.

That was also the first season the Spalding company had the contract to furnish the major-league clubs with their uniforms. In an obvious attempt to make the contract more lucrative, Al Spalding got his friend, president Hulbert, to convince the league that the game needed to add a dash of color through new, more expensive uniforms.

That was how 1882 became the one season in baseball history during which the major-league uniforms could put any softball team's uniforms to shame. Spalding came up with the idea of color-coordinating players by their position in the field. All players wore white pants, belts, and ties, but the color of their caps and shirts signified which position they played.

Pitchers wore baby blue, catchers wore scarlet, shortstops wore maroon, the left fielder wore white, and the right fielder wore grey, while the other positions were combinations of two colors.

How did you tell one team from another? Well, you looked at their stockings, where each club had its own identifying color scheme. The colorful uniforms lasted only one season. It probably didn't take long for someone to point out that it's easy enough to tell a player's position by where he stands in the field.

This crazy experiment managed to leave an impact on the game that is still felt to this day. One result of the color-coded uniforms was to create a lasting tie between a team and the color of its sox. Spalding's team in Chicago became known as the White Sox, and the National League team in Boston, originally known as the Reds, became the first Boston Red Sox!

The Mysterious Death of Big Ed Delahanty

ig Ed was the oldest of the five Delahanty brothers who played in the major leagues. In 1888, the Phillies purchased the minor-league contract of the twenty-year-old second baseman for what was then a record price of $1,900. Delahanty was quickly converted into an outfielder and proved to be worth every penny the Phillies invested in him.

It wasn't long before Big Ed surpassed the legendary Cap Anson as baseball's greatest right-handed hitter. Delahanty finished with a career average of .345, fourth-highest in baseball history. Twice he hit .400, including a .408 batting title in 1899 when he also led the league with 234 hits, 56 doubles, and 134 RBIs. Twice he collected six hits in a game, and once he belted four homers in a single game.

In 1902, Delahanty jumped to the American League and led the circuit in both batting average and slugging percentage. He remains the only batter ever to win batting titles in both the National and American leagues. Delahanty was elected to the Hall of Fame in 1945 despite his career having been suddenly cut short by his untimely and mysterious death at age thirty-five.

In 1903, Ed Delahanty was the American League's defending batting champion and hitting .333 in mid-season. The American and National leagues had just signed a peace treaty which put a cap on player salaries, and on July 2, Delahanty jumped the Washington club to protest the restrictions on his salary. When he was still missing a week later, friends became concerned.

Big Ed Delahanty

The only clues came from a Pullman porter and the night watchman at the International Bridge above Niagara Falls. The Pullman Company had a report of a drunken disturbance aboard a Michigan Central train on the night of July 2. A man reportedly had five drinks and began to terrorize other passengers by waving an open razor. When the train reached Bridgeburg, Canada, the conductor forced the man off. The identity of the drunkard was never established, but the description fit Ed Delahanty.

Later that night, not far from Bridgeburg, the watchman at the International Bridge spotted a man trying to walk across the suspension bridge. He claimed he argued with the man and sent him back to shore.

A week later, on July 9, Ed Delahanty's body was found below Niagara Falls, about twenty miles from the bridge. Had Big Ed fallen from the bridge in a drunken stupor? Some believe the night watchman was covering up the fact that he had accidentally knocked Delahanty off the bridge during a fistfight.

But was Delahanty even the man from the train and the bridge? Perhaps he was simply the victim of a violent robbery and was thrown over the Falls. Often overlooked is the fact that Delahanty's wallet and jewelry were missing from his body. The case is a mystery that will probably never be solved.

Umpire Terrible Tim Hurst

Baseball umpires are expected to endure all kinds of verbal assault, never letting it interfere with their ability to rule impartially and with dignity. At least one umpire never quite got the hang of it. "Terrible" Tim Hurst was probably the most feared and least respected umpire to ever work in the major leagues. Certainly he is the only umpire to be fired by *both* the American and National Leagues.

Terrible Tim began his career in the National League in 1891 at the age of twenty-six. He appeared to know the rules and could tell a ball from a strike, and he certainly had confidence in his judgment. Tim umpired in a cap with the letter "B" on it. When asked why, Tim replied, "It signifies I'm the best."

Not so in the eyes of others who felt Hurst's behavior as an umpire left a lot to be desired. He did not take kindly to players disputing his judgment. If a catcher disagreed too vigorously with a call, Terrible Tim would take off his mask and use it to smack the catcher on the head. And more than once the beefy umpire looked up a player after the game and debated an argument with his fists.

Hurst's career in the National League came to an end in 1897. That summer a fan threw a beer stein that hit Terrible Tim in the back. Hurst calmly picked it up and fired it back into the stands with all his might. The flying tankard beaned an innocent fan, knocking him senseless and setting off a riot.

Amazingly, Hurst then got a job managing the St. Louis Browns. Under his inspired leadership they won 39 games and lost 111. Terrible Tim was fired the next year, and the Browns were so grateful that their record improved by *45* wins!

Seven years after his dismissal in the National League, Hurst was back on the

158

umpire beat, this time in the American League. Terrible Tim's cantankerous style hadn't changed much. One story tells of Yankee manager Clark Griffith stepping on Tim's shoes during an argument; Hurst chased Griffith back to the New York dugout and knocked him out cold.

The end of Terrible Tim's reign of terror came twelve years to the day after he had been banned from the National league. On August 4, 1909, Hurst started a riot by spitting in the eye of Hall of Famer Eddie Collins, the college-bred second baseman for the Philadelphia Athletics.

After his firing, Hurst was asked why he had done it. His only explanation was, "I just don't like college boys." And those college boys had a lot of company in their distaste for Terrible Tim Hurst.

The Black Sox Scandal of 1919

n the early 1900s, gambling on baseball games was a common practice, and more than a few ballplayers were accused of throwing games for monetary gain. This evil practice actually crept into the 1919 World Series, when seven White Sox players agreed to throw the Series to the Cincinnati Reds for $80,000.

The fix nearly fell apart after the first game when the gamblers reneged on their payments. But the final game of the Series was put in the bag when pitcher Lefty Williams and his wife were threatened with bodily harm, possibly

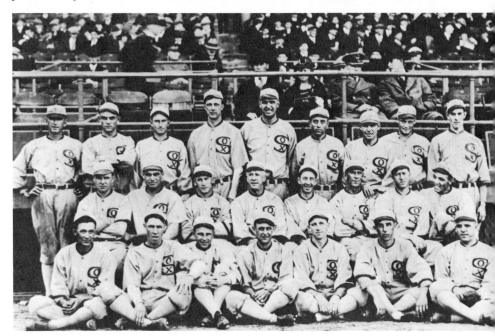

The 1919 Chicago White Sox.

death, if Lefty did not lose the game. Williams gave the game up quickly in the first inning. He gave up four hits to the first five batters and staked the Reds to a four-run lead before leaving the game after only a third of an inning.

Along with the first and final game, the fourth contest was also probably sabotaged by the conspirators. Pitcher Ed Cicotte was in on the fix and made two errors to give the Reds both their runs in a 2-0 victory over the Sox.

There is considerable doubt about the wholehearted participation of Shoeless Joe Jackson, the biggest star in the conspiracy. Obviously, Jackson was tormented by what he had agreed to. After the Series he tried to tell club owner Charles Comiskey what had happened, but Comiskey let him sit for three hours and would not see him. Jackson then tried to return the money and ultimately signed a confession which included the statement that he had played to win. And it's a fact that Jackson led all hitters with a .375 average and hit the only homer of the Series.

But it cannot be denied that Jackson initially agreed to fix the Series and received $5,000 from the gamblers. Eventually the case came before a grand jury which indicted Jackson and the six other conspirators. They played their last game on September 27, 1920. They were tied for first place with the Cleveland Indians, who then left Chicago in the dust after the Sox lost the core of their team. All seven were banished from professional baseball. Shoeless Joe's crime cost him certain election to the Hall of Fame. The same can be said for an eighth player who found himself tied to the conspirators and barred for life from professional baseball.

Buck Weaver, the star third baseman of the White Sox, was asked to join the conspiracy to throw the World Series, but he clearly refused and did not receive a dime from the gamblers. He went on to play brilliantly in the Series where he hit .324 and led all players with five extra-base hits.

The fact that Weaver refused to squeal on his teammates was considered normal, even honorable, according to the morals of that era. But Weaver was the first player barred for life under a ruling that penalizes any player who fails to report being approached about fixing a game.

As unfair as it may have seemed at the time, the sweeping penalties against the Black Sox and Buck Weaver spelled an end to gambling's evil hold on the national pastime.

Baseball Nicknames

oes any sport have more fascinating nicknames than baseball? Okay, it gets a little boring when about two hundred major leaguers have been nicknamed "Lefty," but what about guys like Kickapoo Summers, Ping Bodie, Chicken Wolf, Jazzbow Buskey, Icebox Chamberlain, Oil Can Boyd, Bad News Galloway, and Boog Powell?

Lots of times baseball nicknames are supposed to tell us something about the player. Fleat Clifton, Tom Thumb Forest, and Half-Pint Rye were obviously little guys. Bones Barker, String Grandy, Stick Michael, and Mark "The Blade" Belanger were on the skinny side. And Butterball Botz, Hippo Vaughn, and Whale Walters all had something in common with Ron "The Round Man" Northley —who packed over 200 pounds on a five-foot-ten-inch frame.

We are led to believe that Wagon Tongue Adams and Earache Meyer never shut up, and Boob McNair, Puddin' Head Jones, Do Do Armstrong, Possum Whitted, and Bozo Cicotte were not Rhodes scholars. Things are pretty clear about a pitcher named Glass Arm Brown and Al Orth "The Curveless Wonder." And it's an educated guess that slow-running catcher Maytag Malone ran like a washing machine.

Sometimes the connection isn't as clear. Was Bootnose Hoffman kicked in the face? What's the story behind Available Jones and Desperate Desmond Beatty? Were Pooch Barnhart, Fido Baldwin, and Bow Wow Arft really dogs? And what were they trying to tell us about the batch of major leaguers known as Lady Baldwin, Mary Calhoun, Beverly Bain, Daisy Davis, Zsa Zsa Harvey, Dolly Gray, Patsy Cahill, and Baby Doll Jacobson?

Some nicknames have a well-known ring to them. King Lear, Stonewall Jackson, Kaiser Wilhelm, Sarah Bernhardt, and Flash Gordon all played in the major leagues. Some nicknames find their appeal in a simply rhyme: Goober Zoober, Steady Eddie Brinkman, Slow Joe Doyle, Stan the Man Musial, and Downtown Brown.

Some of the best nicknames have come from a play off the last name—Ding Dong Bell, Dusty Rhodes, Rainbow Trout, Leaky Faucet, and Bud Weiser.

Baseball's fascination with the fastball has led to several creative efforts such as Cannonball Crane, Bullet Joe Bush, Sudden Sam McDowell, The Hoosier Thunderbolt (Amos Rusie), The Big Train (Walter Johnson), and Louisiana Lightning (Ron Guidry).

Not everyone was happy with their nicknames. Losing Pitcher Mulcahy, Stinky Davis, and Swamp Baby Donald probably preferred their given names of Hugh, Harry, and Atley. Baseball historians tend to lean toward the old outfielder Cactus Gavvy Cravath as having baseball's best nickname, but the winner here is an Oakland pitcher from the 1960s and 1970s. His parents christened him Johnny Lee but we all came to know him as Blue Moon Odom, a name that sings on the tongue and sticks in the memory.

Sabotage and the Spitball

B ack in the Dead-Ball Era, when the spitball was a legal pitch, some pitchers had a less-than-savory method of applying saliva to the ball. Ed Walsh, who established the spitball in the major leagues, started off using a technique in which he actually licked the ball rather than spitting on it or on his fingers.

In 1909 the Philadelphia Athletics broke him of that habit by smearing the ball with a little horse manure. Walsh lost his lunch and then fired a string of beanballs as the guilty parties came to the plate.

Well, the City of Brotherly Love had another baseball team, and in 1912 the Philadelphia Phillies gave the Athletics' strategy a new twist when they decided to sabotage a similar spitballer from Pittsburgh named Marty O'Toole.

It was first baseman Fred Luderus who decided his team ought to take advantage of O'Toole's habit of licking the ball. Luderus got a tube of red-hot liniment and coated the inside of his glove with it. Every time he handled the ball some of the liniment was transferred to the ball and eventually to O'Toole's tongue. By the third inning O'Toole's tongue was so raw and inflamed that he had to be removed from the game.

Pirates manager Fred Clarke figured out what had happened and protested to the umpires that putting liniment on the ball·was illegal as well as a threat to his pitcher's health. Charlie "Red" Dooin, the Phillies manager, liked the health argument and countered, "Every time he spits on the ball we're going to disinfect it. There's nothing that says we don't have a right to protect *our* health."

The umpires neatly sidestepped the protest by pointing out that O'Toole was already out of the game and a pitch had been thrown before the Pirates figured out what the Phillies had done. Technically it was too late to file a protest, but the umpires promised to refer the problem to the league office.

While most of the participants found the incident on the humorous side, the National League president was not amused. He ordered all teams to cease and desist from using this unique defense against O'Toole's spitball.

O'Toole went on to have his best year and led the league in shutouts. But you have to wonder if he was ever able to look at another ball without suspicion.

Marty O'Toole

INDEX

Note: **boldface** page numbers indicate photographs.